T0670876

# simplifying
# THE SOUL

Paula Huston's new book is very much like the author herself: wise, compassionate, patient, friendly, inviting. Her warm and personal series of meditations will surely draw you more deeply into the great mystery of Lent. Too often thought of as simply a season of sacrifice, Lent is revealed here as something far richer—a privileged time to experience God in your everyday life, to open yourself to conversion, and to savor God's transforming love.

**James Martin, S.J.**
Author of *The Jesuit Guide to (Almost) Everything*

This is the most moving, most appealing and, at the same time, most practical book I have ever seen on Lenten practices. It is a verbal retreat that invites both the soul and the body to a holy retooling.

**Phyllis Tickle**
Author of *The Great Emergence*

Paula Huston takes a series of simple, ordinary acts—the first is to clean out a junk drawer—inserts it into a brief personal story, and turns it into a Lenten practice. One act and story for each day of Lent. She offers herself as a lively companion in a Lenten practice stripped of clichés. Join her—it might be the simplest and liveliest Lent you have ever kept.

**Eugene Peterson**
Author of *Pastor: A Memoir*

Paula Huston, a natural storyteller, is also a woman of finely honed spiritual intelligence. I love that the practices she recommends are eminently doable, rising out of the down-to-earth lifestyle she and her husband have chosen. When I read her words I am galvanized and motivated toward greater simplicity.

**Luci Shaw**
Author of *Water My Soul*

Simple, yet so profound! Paula Huston provides spiritual seekers a fresh perspective on the opportunities opened to us during the season of Lent. By pairing enlightened meditations with practical disciplines, Paula leads us to a renewed soul, a space for a deeper relationship with Christ, and an inner room to revel in the promises of Easter. Simply beautiful!

**Lisa M. Hendey**
Author of *The Handbook for Catholic Moms*

Paula Huston is one of my favorite guides to a fuller spiritual life. She's so sane, sympathetic, and practical, recognizing that the way to holiness need not be as daunting or difficult as we sometimes make it seem. *Simplifying the Soul* draws on monastic wisdom and the inspiration of the desert fathers to emphasize again that easy, improving practices that give us greater calm and happiness may be exactly what God wishes for us in our Lenten season.

**Ron Hansen**
Author of *Mariette in Ecstasy*

# simplifying
# THE SOUL

*Lenten Practices to Renew Your Spirit*

## PAULA HUSTON

ave maria press AMP notre dame, indiana

Excerpts by Thomas Merton from *The Wisdom of the Desert*, copyright © 1960 by The Abbey of Gethsemani, Inc., reprinted by permission of New Directions Publishing Corp.

Excerpts from *The Praktikos and Chapters on Prayer*, copyright © 1972 by Cistercian Publications, reprinted by permission of Liturgical Press, licensee of Cistercian Publications.

Excerpts from *The Sayings of the Desert Fathers*, copyright © 1975 by Benedicta Ward, reprinted by permission of Liturgical Press, licensee of Cistercian Publications.

Scripture texts used in this work are taken from the *New American Bible* copyright © 1991, 1986, and 1970 by the Confraternity of Christian Doctrine, Washington, DC, and are used by permission of the copyright owner. All rights reserved. No part of the *New American Bible* may be reproduced in any form or by any means without permission in writing from the publisher.

---

© 2011 by Paula Huston

All rights reserved. No part of this book may be used or reproduced in any manner whatsoever, except in the case of reprints in the context of reviews, without written permission from Ave Maria Press®, Inc., P.O. Box 428, Notre Dame, IN 46556.

Founded in 1865, Ave Maria Press is a ministry of the United States Province of Holy Cross.

www.avemariapress.com

ISBN-10 1-59471-269-7    ISBN-13 978-1-59471-269-2

Cover image © Alloy Photography.

Cover and text design by Katherine J. Ross.

Printed and bound in the United States of America.

*Library of Congress Cataloging-in-Publication Data*

Huston, Paula.
  Simplifying the soul : Lenten practices to renew your spirit / Paula Huston.
    p. cm.
  Includes bibliographical references (p.).
  ISBN-13: 978-1-59471-269-2 (pbk.)
  ISBN-10: 1-59471-269-7 (pbk.)
  1. Lent. 2. Simplicity--Religious aspects--Catholic Church. 3. Spiritual life--Catholic Church.  I. Title.
  BV85.H87 2011
  242'.34--dc23

                                                    11025246

green press INITIATIVE

Dedicated to the memory of
**Father Bernard Massicotte, O.S.B. Cam.**
(July 1, 1928–May 25, 2011),
whose unfailing love, wise guidance,
and elvish sense of humor gently conquered
my resistance to the faith.

# CONTENTS

# INTRODUCTION

Though spiritual growth occurs in all kinds of different settings, my own development has been strongly shaped by years of being an oblate, or lay associate of a monastic community. The monks, their routines, and even the grounds of the monastery are so familiar to me now that each visit feels like a homecoming. Yet no matter how well I have come to know the place, and no matter what condition I'm in when I arrive, each time I return to it, I'm startled by the same phenomenon, one that always catches me off guard. I'm surprised anew by the knowledge that I'm once again undergoing a spiritual "recalibration." The mechanism of my soul is, in a very real way, being cleaned, repaired, and reset. When it's time to leave, I'm in a better state.

When I began pondering what quality of the hermitage triggers this process in me, I realized that, to a large degree, it is the simplicity of the place. Though the Big Sur wilderness setting is shockingly beautiful, its beauty is not distracting; there is a solidity, clarity, and predictability in untrammeled nature that I find immensely soothing. Deer graze, unafraid, outside my trailer. Squirrels run across my roof. The winds blow, the rains come, the fog drifts in, the sun rises and sets. Bells call me to prayer time, celebrated four times daily and always at the same hour. Food is basic but nourishing, accommodations minimalist but comfortable. Relationships are limited to warm glances, smiles, brief whispered conversations outside the chapel, or scheduled confession and spiritual direction.

For the space of a few days, I am released from the bondage of complexity. Amazingly, those few days are enough to help me find my way back to the image of Jesus trudging before me in his dusty sandals, the man with no place to lay his head. The sense of joy and relief at once again taking my place in the crowd behind him is palpable. And as usual, until I arrive at the hermitage, I have no idea of how far I have once again strayed off the path.

Instead of humbly following along behind Jesus, I've let myself get sidetracked by a myriad of temptations: overly ambitious creative projects, delusions about my own importance, worrisome relationships, secret small addictions, stubborn resentments, and a hundred forms of self-indulgence. The simple life of the hermitage clears my vision enough to see how far I've wandered. This is a humbling experience.

For centuries, the Church has practiced a lengthy annual version of my short monastic retreats. We call it Lent, the season of the year that is particularly devoted to introspection, compunction (a piercing sense of regret for sinning), and repentance. Lent begins on Ash Wednesday, when people go to church to have their foreheads crossed with ashes, the traditional symbol of mourning. These ashes come from the burnt fronds of the previous year's Palm Sunday, and are meant to be a visible reminder of the seriousness of Lenten practice. The season officially ends at sundown on Holy Thursday, and is followed by the glorious miracle of the Triduum: the Last Supper, the passion, and the resurrection of Christ. During Lent, we deliberately strive to bring on the spiritual recalibration that takes me by surprise each time I go to the hermitage. The purpose is the same, however: a simplification of soul (today, we might more readily use the term "self," though this term does not capture the spiritual element of our personhood) that fosters the development of humility.

For centuries, humility was seen as a key component of a healthy spiritual life. In more recent times, humility has lost a good deal of status. Instead, we prefer to focus on the development of self-esteem, on achievement, and on self-fulfillment; our temptation is to dismiss humility as a relic of the unsophisticated past, a time when people supposedly knew next to nothing about psychology or good mental health. We also tend to link the promotion of humility with authoritarian efforts to keep people passively disinclined to rock the boat.

Yet scripture is filled with references to humility, from the Beatitudes that open the Sermon on the Mount ("Blessed are the poor in spirit, for theirs is the kingdom of heaven; blessed are the meek, for they shall inherit the land") to

Jesus' declaration that unless we become like little children we cannot enter the kingdom (Mt 5:3, 5). St. Benedict of Nursia, founder of the Benedictine order, devotes the longest chapters in his famous Rule to the subject of humility and considers the journey toward humility to be one and the same as the journey toward Christlikeness.

Truly humble people are grounded in reality; they neither preen under illusions of greatness nor suffer agonies of self-hatred. As Benedictine Mary Margaret Funk points out, "The practice of humility is to be neither too high or too low" in our self-estimation.[1] Freed from the terrible frustrations that accompany idealistic perfectionism or moral scrupulosity, we quietly accept the truth of who we are: weak human beings, prone to fail and tempted toward evil, yet at the same time, filled with an almost unbearable longing for goodness, love, and intimacy with God.

What are the attributes of humility? Not surprisingly, they are the very same "fruits of the Spirit" we find listed in scripture: love, joy, peace, patience, kindness, generosity, faithfulness, gentleness, and self-control. Humility renders us transparent to others and opens our hearts to grace and the workings of the Holy Spirit. It is what allows us to obey Jesus' double commandment: "You shall love the Lord, your God, with all your heart, with all your soul, and with all your mind. . . . You shall love your neighbor as yourself" (Mt 22:37, 39). Humility provides the seedbed for holiness.

Growth in humility, however, doesn't come naturally. As human beings, we are woefully tempted toward self-elevation (vainglory), and stony withdrawal from God and our fellow creatures (pride), along with a myriad of other sins no less destructive (gluttony, lust, greed, envy, self-pitying depression over what we want and can't have, simmering resentment, anger). Not dealt with, such sins fill us with hopelessness and confusion, and drastically complicate our relationships. They keep us focused on our selves, block our ability to love, and isolate us from God.

As a wise friend of mine says, "Sin is complicated." The obverse of this little rule is that humility, the ground of goodness, is simple and open.

The beauty of the Lenten season is that it encourages the development of a humble heart. In Lent, we are invited to look deeply inside, identify what is impeding our ability to follow Christ along the path of humility, and begin applying antidotes. Early church tradition is rich in the wisdom of soul simplification and offers a multitude of spiritual disciplines to counteract the temptations that muddle our lives. The season of Lent gives us the opportunity to devote significant time to this endeavor.

*Simplifying the Soul* is meant to aid you in this process. Structured as an individual retreat, it presents daily readings that begin on Ash Wednesday and end on Holy Thursday. Following tradition, it does not include Sundays, which have always been seen as mini-celebrations of the resurrection. Each reading from Jesus and the Desert Fathers and Mothers is in some way tied to the development of humility. Since we learn (and change) by doing, each day of the retreat is also devoted to a different action you might take to help you along the path. Many of these suggestions come straight out of Catholic practice (you might recognize the corporal works of mercy, for example, along with the practice of the virtues), but others are adaptations of old wisdom woven into contemporary life (cleaning out a junk drawer, giving up TV for a day, walking to the grocery store instead of driving, etc.).

Each activity is designed to be completed in a single day with the hope that some of them will prove so helpful you'll incorporate them into your daily, post-Lenten practice. Others may need to be modified because you are dealing with special circumstances; if this is your situation, it is surely better to try a reduced version of the suggested activity than to skip it altogether. Still others may not seem to apply to your life at all; for example, perhaps you have no computer, so can't very well stop e-mailing for a day. In this case, read the meditation, then use your imagination to come up with a suitable alternative.

The benefits of adopting such disciplines, even if only temporarily, are twofold. First, they twitch back the curtain on hidden sin. For example, fasting immediately reveals our secret propensity toward gluttony (today, we would probably refer to this as bingeing), and shutting off the computer for a time brings us face to face with our unacknowledged addiction to constant stimulation. We are guaranteed to be surprised at what we learn about ourselves when we deliberately attempt to break an old habit. Despite our tendency to dismiss premodern thinkers as psychologically unsophisticated, many of them demonstrated a profound grasp of the psyche and its wily games.

Second, such disciplines give us a way to counteract life-complicating temptations. Deliberately, we do the opposite of what feels natural and desirable. And if we're able to carry through, we experience the lifting of a burden and the clearing of a horizon. Life becomes simpler, and we experience, perhaps for the first time, a measure of real self-acceptance—one of the hallmarks of humility. To be sure, these small ascetical experiments make us cognizant of our weakness, but at the same time, they reveal to us the depth of our longing for God and for goodness. Just as my periodic "recalibration" at the hermitage enables me to calm down and focus, these daily exercises in soul simplification point us back to our real priority—following Christ—and help us get on with the journey.

My prayer for you as you begin this retreat is that, first of all, you enter into it with the right spirit. This book is not meant to be a spiritual version of the Girl Scout honor badge program, and if you look upon it as a handbook for self-improvement, you'll more than likely become frustrated and disappointed. Instead, think of it as an invitation to self-knowledge and as a small step in liberation from destructive complicatedness—that is, from sin.

Second, I pray that if you plan to take on the project, you'll commit to the entire retreat and carry through to the end. A truism about spiritual disciplines is that they only work when they are faithfully practiced. Even when you are not drawn to a particular activity, I hope you will give it a try. Almost invariably, the most unpalatable action will often prove to be the very antidote you've been seeking.

Finally, I hope that somewhere along the line you'll experience a conversion of the heart that outlasts these seven weeks of Lent. As Michael Casey puts it,

> Conversion means being liberated by God's grace so that we can at last follow the intimate spiritual aspirations that have long been unheeded, neglected, or frustrated. It is the beginning of the journey towards a fulfillment, a journey powered by the spiritual quest but one which profoundly influences and transforms every sphere of human activity and experience.[2]

I hope with all my heart that you might experience the grace of conversion and the gift of greater humility during this coming Lent.

# beginnings:
## SIMPLIFYING SPACE

The desert dwellers used the image of a muddy pond or dirty mirror to describe a mind cluttered by distraction. They believed that what we cling to says a lot about the state of our souls. Their beliefs were rooted in Jesus' injunctions to stay focused on the one true thing—the pearl of great price, the treasure in the field.

## Ash Wednesday: Clear Out a Junk Drawer or Closet

*Abbot Pastor said: If you have a chest full of clothing, and leave it for a long time, the clothing will rot inside it. It is the same with the thoughts in our heart. If we do not carry them out by physical action, after awhile, they will spoil and turn bad.*[1]

### MEDITATION

Recently, we moved from our rambling old place to a new one in the back of our property. We call the new place Acorn House. The two living spaces, one showing its scars and the other still smelling like lumber and fresh paint, sit 317 feet apart; they are connected by a trail that meanders through the pines and—in springtime—heaps of blue lupine. We have been on these four acres for twenty-five years. Acorn House is meant to shelter us through the next quarter century while our grandchildren, we hope, grow up as our children did: in the big battered house on the hill.

In this new little home, built for two, there are more windows than walls. A spectacular view gives us a sense of space we really don't have. Though there's a second bedroom and bath upstairs, we're committed to living on the first floor only, saving the upstairs for guests or someday a caregiver. Our goal in building the house this way was twofold: we were looking for a way to live more simply but also more contemplatively—that is, more deeply connected to God. In this case, our connection to God was strengthened by the peaceful beauty of nature. And so our life of twenty-five years has been shrink-wrapped into 925 square feet that includes a single bedroom closet, a few cupboards and drawers in the kitchen, and a slender pantry, lined with shelves.

In a house this size, there's no leftover space for a random junk drawer. Yet we had plenty of them in the old place—crannies stuffed with unrelated items, some of them easily tossed but others evocative of life phases weathered and nearly forgotten. What were we to do with these stashes when it was time to move?

My husband's initial response was to pull his favorite junk drawer from a nightstand we were leaving behind and carry it through the woods to the new house where it sat on the floor beside the bed for several weeks. Though I was sorely tempted to cart it away, I instead decided to wait for Mike to surrender to our new reality; the days of heedless squirreling were over. Everything we carried on into the future had to be essential. Eventually, he accepted this fact. One day, the drawer disappeared.

The great third- and fourth-century flight made by thousands of Christians into the Egyptian and Syrian deserts stemmed in part from a similar impulse: to strip, to cull, and to give away or eliminate anything that might tie one to the past. The Desert Fathers and Mothers were on a quest for purity of heart, and they understood that physical items are never just themselves but rather symbols and reminders of the life we must, however reluctantly, be willing to relinquish if we are ever to change.

Mary Margaret Funk points out that the narrow way Jesus describes in the gospels involves a fourfold renunciation, the first of which is giving up our former way of life. We must be willing to undergo what she calls *conversatio morum*, or ongoing conversion.[2] This process necessarily involves breaking our strong emotional ties to the familiar (and comfortable) past and turning our faces, with however much trepidation, toward an unknown future.

A junk drawer is the classic repository for what we are meant to leave behind. Not only does it symbolize our histories, but it also reveals the speed at which we lived through them: how did a sunflower seed wind up among the rubber bands and old corks, and this seventy-five-year-old baptismal gown stuffed into a brown paper sack?

When we clean out a junk drawer for Lent, we are in some small way dealing with the detritus of breathless hurry and our corresponding inability to focus. We are beginning to tear through the sticky web that binds us to our past: not only to the fine and happy times, the poignant seasons of growth and change, but also to the tears we once shed, the idols we once worshipped, the myths we once believed, and the lies we once told ourselves.

### PRACTICE

On this first day of Lent, spend some time going through a favorite stash, asking yourself what these items represent. Many of them will no doubt qualify as genuine junk, things that were simply stuck away instead of being carried out to the trash. Others might be useful, except for the fact that they are never used; these are easily bequeathed to someone else. If you come across something you cannot yet bear to part with, don't struggle with yourself too long. Instead, pack it in a box, label it, and seal it up; then store it in an attic or the garage rafters for a few years, remembering that, if you leave it there too long, someone else will have to deal with it. Meanwhile, pray for liberation from these ultimately ephemeral reminders of the past.

> Everyone who listens to these words of mine and acts on them will be like a wise man who built his house on rock. (Mt 7:24)

## Thursday: Scrub a Dirty Corner

*An Elder was once asked when the soul acquires humility. He answered, "When it thinks about its own vices."* [3]

### MEDITATION

As we began the job of transferring furniture and appliances to the new house, hidden pockets of grime began to materialize all over the place we'd lived in for twenty-five years. At first, I cringed with embarrassment. I then moved to defensiveness. After all, who in her right mind regularly scrubs behind the microwave? Cleans the oven? Even bothers to glance at the top of the refrigerator?

The great irony was this: like my Norwegian grandmothers before me, I have always been what they once called "house proud." I make sure that linen closets are maintained in a rational order, that dishes get washed and stacked each night, and that wandering pens, newspapers, bills, and socks are firmly corralled within their proper places the moment they dare stray into the public arena. Yet, unlike those Norwegian grandmothers, when it comes to hidden grime, my philosophy has always been "out of sight, out of mind."

Others have noticed: my mother-in-law, who on our honeymoon got after the "slurpage" beneath the veggie crisper in the fridge; my Dutch aunt, who stayed with us a week and spent much of it ferreting out greasy dust balls under the stove; and our daughter Kelly, who moved back in for a few months between jobs and assigned to herself the role of window track scrubber. For them, it was the hidden dirt that inspired their zeal.

I had to wonder: how could I obsess about surface messiness but blithely ignore concealed potential health hazards? And did this propensity toward shoring up appearances at the expense of getting after what was deep and hidden extend, perhaps, to my spiritual life? The appalling grime revealed during our move inspired me to revisit this question. And I had to admit that the answer was yes; the same dynamic was clearly at work in me when it came to, for example, confession.

For years, two patient priests, first Fr. Bernard and then Fr. Isaiah, have listened to long, funny stories, fielded earnest theoretical questions, and been subjected to cartloads of charm but heard very few genuine confessions from me.

Confession still makes me uneasy: it is all about exposing the most hidden, shameful aspects of myself to another human being. And the only time I am willing to go through it is when keeping those secrets is more painful than the embarrassment of revealing what I've so diligently pushed out of sight and out of mind.

This tendency to ignore spiritual problems that are not readily apparent is not unique to me, however, and is the reason that ancient monasticism developed a practice of manifesting one's thoughts to a spiritual elder (in Greek, *gerontin*; in Russian, *startzey*). Elders were people who had been transformed, who could see beyond surface appearance, and who could "read" hearts with an eerie clairvoyance that brooked no weaseling attempts to look good rather than be good. Would-be monks were advised to "become, brother, like the camel. Bearing your imperfections, let your spiritual guide, who knows the way better than you, direct you on the path to God."[4]

The act of physically scrubbing out a dirty corner, especially one that is hidden, can be a helpful reminder of our preference for life on the shining surface. And the humility required to get down in the muck this way, taking on an onerous job the results of which few will ever notice, helps point us in a new direction, toward life in the light of the Spirit.

But none of this is easy. Psalm 19 recognizes our difficulties in dealing with concealed sin, which we can easily ignore for so long we lose awareness of its presence: "Who can detect heedless failings? Cleanse me from my unknown faults." The great blessing of genuine confession is that God will manifest our secret sins to us if only we will ask. And then, in his infinite merciful love, he will forgive us and make us clean.

### PRACTICE

Today, spend a little time thinking about a particularly unappealing cleaning job you have been putting off. If it's too big to accomplish in an hour or so, leave it aside till after Lent. Instead, choose a task small enough to invalidate any claims that you don't have time to do it. Maybe you'll choose the cupboard under the kitchen sink, that classic repository of cleaning-product–wet-sponge goo. Maybe, instead, you will scrub behind a toilet. Whatever you choose, however, take it slowly and deliberately, looking hard at what time and neglect have wrought.

When you're done—and here's the tough part—resist the temptation to point out your hard work to anyone, especially your spouse. Instead, in the privacy of your heart, pray for the gift of discernment regarding hidden sin, and for the grace of forgiveness.

> I tell you . . . there will be more joy in heaven over one sinner who repents than over ninety-nine righteous people who have no need of repentance. (Lk 15:7)

## Friday: Give Away Something You Are Not Using

*Abba Theodore of Pherme had acquired three good books. He came to Abba Macarius and said to him, "I have three excellent books from which I derive profit; the brethren also make use of them and derive profit from them. Tell me what I ought to do; keep them for my use and that of the brethren, or sell them and give the money to the poor?" The old man answered him in this way, "Your actions are good; but it is best of all to possess nothing." Hearing that, he went and sold his books and gave the money for them to the poor.*[5]

### MEDITATION

I wrote my first novel in my early forties. The story of a gifted young pianist, it required me to have much more knowledge of music than I in fact had, so I relied heavily on research and the input of Tina, my professional pianist sister. It was she who convinced me that my protagonist should choose Beethoven's last piano sonata as her recital centerpiece. As Tina put it, "It's sort of a legend that nobody can play both movements equally well."

My goal as I wrote the book was to enter so deeply into the world of piano performance that readers would be convinced I was a real musician. I bought a small cassette player and headphones (this was the early nineties), and every time I worked on the novel during the next two years, Alfred

Brendel's version of Opus 111 was pouring into my ears as I wrote. After the novel was published, I stuck the tape away and pretty much forgot about it. Once or twice a year, I would dig around until I found it, look at it fondly, and then perhaps listen to it for a few minutes before sticking it away again. Though I considered it one of my most precious possessions, it was no longer of much use to me.

One day, a Russian friend called to see whether a visiting group of Orthodox Christians might spend the day relaxing at our house between concerts. "They're tired," she told me, "and they need some peace and quiet and maybe a good meal if you've got the time." I said yes, that was fine, and a few weeks later she deposited five young Russians at our front door.

We ate, we talked, and then Andrei, a violinist, asked if he could look through my music collection. Of course, I told him, and soon he had pulled out the Alfred Brendel tape. "I've never heard this one before," he said, excited. "Could I please listen?"

As the achingly familiar music began to flood the room, I could see him going into a trance. Eyes closed, swaying, fingers drumming against his knees, he'd clearly entered Beethoven's mental space, and I realized I must have looked much the same during those years of sitting at the computer with my headphones on, trying to negotiate an unfamiliar universe.

Just as the music ended, my friend arrived to pick them up for the next concert. Andrei looked stricken. "Oh, I wish there was time to hear it again," he said. "The whole thing!" For a moment I hesitated, and then I thrust it into his hands. "Take it back to Russia," I said. "Please. Play it for your fellow musicians."

The Desert Fathers and Mothers understood that clinging to possessions, no matter how precious or beautiful, is a form of servitude. We cannot move easily when we are burdened by the things, however lovely, we carry on our backs. The desert dwellers' radical divestment of earthly goods later inspired St. Benedict, the father of Western monasticism, to take a firm stance against owning anything at all.

In his famous Rule, written in the sixth century, he has this to say about shedding possessions:

> Above all, this evil practice must be uprooted and removed from the monastery. We mean that without an order from the abbot, no one may presume to give, receive, or retain anything on his own, nothing at all—not a book, writing tablets, or stylus—in short, not a single item, especially since monks may not have free disposal even of their own bodies and wills. . . . All things should be the common possession of all, as it is written, so that no one presumes to call anything his own (Acts 4:32).[6]

Though it hurt to give away that cassette tape, so rich in sentimental value, it felt better in the long run to know it was now in the hands of young Andrei. As precious as it had been to me, it was, after all, only a thing.

### PRACTICE

Today, give away something you are not using, preferably something to which you are emotionally attached. If you can, give it to the person who could most benefit by its presence in his or her life. Pray for this person, and also for yourself, that you might taste the sweetness of being liberated from the seductive tyranny of beautiful possessions.

> When Jesus saw a crowd around him, he gave orders to cross to the other side. A scribe approached and said to him, "Teacher, I will follow you wherever you go."
>
> Jesus answered him, "Foxes have dens and birds of the sky have nests, but the Son of Man has nowhere to rest his head." (Mt 8:18–20)

## Saturday: Set Up a Special Place of Prayer

*Abbot Pastor said, "Any trial whatever that comes to you can be conquered by silence."* [7]

### MEDITATION

Twenty years ago, with our four kids all in their early teens, I'd given up on ever finding a quiet retreat at home. Then, for my birthday, Mike built me a bench on the big, pine-covered hill that takes up half our property. I'd always loved the hush of that forest but, up till then, there'd been nowhere to sit without sledding down the thick needles that blanketed the slope. With my new bench in place under a magnificent Torrey pine, I began a daily practice of silence at dawn.

Much as I reveled in the sheer pleasure of this unaccustomed quiet, I soon became aware that something more than mere silence was going on. Secret and mysterious, it had the feel of prayer without words. I'd always assumed that "real" prayer was petitionary: you raised your concerns with God, you asked him for various worthwhile things, and you begged him for forgiveness. Yet, as I sat each day in the rose-colored light, I didn't feel like making petitions at all. What was going on here?

Then I read a little book by André Louf called *Teach Us to Pray*, and I found my explanation. Louf says, "We received prayer along with grace, at our baptism. The state of grace as we call it, at the level of the heart, actually signifies a state of prayer. . . . This state of prayer within us is something we always carry about, like a hidden treasure of which we are not consciously aware—or hardly so. Somewhere our heart is going full pelt, but we do not feel it."[8]

My early morning sits on the bench set the tone each day for my otherwise fast-paced life as wife, mother, writer, and university teacher. The practice helped me get through the next busy decade, at which time I was finally able to give up my teaching job in search of a simpler and more prayerful life at home. In honor of my early retirement, Mike asked me where I'd like to build a writing studio, and, of course, I chose the site under the Torrey pine where for so long my forest bench had stood.

I'll find the same peace and quiet inside the new studio, I told myself. The bench can go—it's okay. When we were done building, I hung icons, put up a cross and bought a meditation cushion; I assured myself that it might take a little while to get used to the change of venue, but essentially, everything was the same.

It was not. The writing studio was for writing, not for silent prayer. It housed my library of spiritual books—wonderful books but filled with words that got my mind to spinning. The simplicity of the bench was gone and, with it, my ability to hear my organ of prayer "going full pelt."

Eight more years went by. Then came the day we moved into our new little house in the oak trees, and when I woke up on the first morning, I walked out onto the front porch and realized I was looking straight into the sunrise. I pulled up a rocker and sat down to listen. And sure enough, just as on that long-ago dawn bench, there it was again, hushed and mysterious, like the gushing of a hidden interior spring: my secretly praying heart.

### PRACTICE

Perhaps you live in a crowded apartment with little space and even less privacy. Or maybe you are surrounded by neighbors in the suburbs. As difficult as it is to find a spot you can call your own, try to identify a place on a balcony or in your yard where you might sit in uninterrupted quiet for at least fifteen minutes each day.

Make it special. Set up a chair or bench that will stay in place. Make sure you can look at something beautiful when you are spending time here: a flowering tree or shrub, a view of the sky. If you cannot find anything appropriate at home, consider a nearby park bench. You do not have to own it to make it yours.

> Blessed are the eyes that see what you see. For I say to you, many prophets and kings desired to see what you see, but did not see it, and to hear what you hear, but did not hear it. (Lk 10:23–24)

# first week of lent:
## SIMPLIFYING THE USE OF MONEY

The desert dwellers took Christ's words to the rich young man literally—if you want to follow me, give away everything you have. Jesus reiterated in many different ways that it is impossible to serve two masters: God and mammon, love and self-indulgence.

### Monday: Make a Meal from Stored or Forgotten Items

*The disciple of a certain Elder went to fetch water from the well, which was about three hours distant from their hut. When he arrived there, he remembered that he had not taken the rope with him.*

*"Lord, help me in my need, through the prayers of my holy Elder," the young man prayed, having faith in God and trust in the powers of his Abba.*

*With surprise he then saw the water rise to the rim
of the well. When he had filled his vessels, the water
again descended to its normal depth.*[1]

### MEDITATION

Mike and I talked about building a new house for years,
but we never had the money to begin. Our life savings was
tied up in a small rental a few miles away, our "golden egg,"
as Mike fondly called it. As retirees, our income was limited,
but as long as we had the rental, we had something we could
sell when we were finally ready to build, or (worst-case sce-
nario) if times ever got really tough.

In 2007, they did: the housing market went into a nose-
dive just as our oldest daughter and her husband, who'd
been living a thousand miles away, began seriously thinking about moving their young family closer to grandparents.
Under normal circumstances, they could have lived in the
rental until they found jobs. However, the real estate crisis,
followed by the worst recession in decades, convinced us
that we needed to cash in our golden egg as quickly as possible. So instead of inviting the kids to move in, we gave
notice to the renters who were already there, put the place
up for sale, and then watched in shock as its value plum-
meted by tens of thousands of dollars. Worse, as month after
month went by with no rent money coming in, we began
slipping into serious debt. The anxiety burned inside my gut
and kept me awake at night.

But the place finally sold. Though we wound up with far less than we might have two years before, we were thrilled to once more be solvent. For a few months, we reveled in the unfamiliar experience of having enough money in the bank. Though the recession had not yet eased, we urged the kids to make the long-delayed move—they could live with us until they got settled—and when they arrived, we began working on the plans for our long-dreamed-of, small and simple retirement house in the oaks at the back of the property.

What we didn't know before we began is that building from scratch, no matter what size the place, is like turning on a money faucet full blast. No matter how many of the tasks we handled ourselves, the costs mounted at a dizzying rate. Worse, the recession had seemingly destroyed the job market for teachers; despite their best efforts, our daughter and her husband could not find decent work. Soon, we had not only burned through all our "golden egg" profits, we had to go out shopping for a new mortgage. Things once again felt very shaky, and I found myself becoming increasingly fearful about the future. Were we about to lose everything after all?

One day in prayer, however, it came to me that this anxious insecurity was blinding me to the wealth God *had* provided us: our health, our almost-finished house, our beloved daughter and son-in-law, our young grandchildren, our neighbors, and our land. We might not have money in the bank, but we were knee-deep in blessings. In his classic work *Self-Abandonment to Divine Providence*, J. P. de Caussade says, "The present moment is always full of infinite treasures, it contains far more than you have the capacity to hold. Faith is the measure; what you find in the present moment will be according to the measure of your faith."[2]

On our first night in the new house, we slept on a mattress on the floor. The rest of the furniture had not yet been moved, but I'd brought down the pots and pans and dishes, and I was determined to make a real meal despite the fact that I hadn't had a chance yet to stock up on food. We'd been working so hard on the construction project that everything else had gone by the wayside.

Resisting the automatic impulse to drive to the store—it seemed important, somehow, to put this feast together with what was on hand—I instead headed out to our long-neglected garden, guessing I might find some overlooked provisions. Sure enough, there was a lush head of blue-green spring broccoli hidden among the weeds. Digging around in the crabgrass-choked potato patch, I came upon a trove of tender fingerlings. But it was the barn freezer that yielded up the best find of all—a long-forgotten turkey breast, perfect for the Thanksgiving-style repast that followed.

### PRACTICE

As a way to become more aware of overlooked blessings, take some time today to plan and cook a meal entirely from stored items. Check out the refrigerator, the freezer, and the highest shelves in the pantry. As you gather your supplies, ask yourself why these particular items have been sitting around for so long. Were you overly focused on being prepared for every occasion? Are your shelves jammed with duplicates? How do your food-buying habits reflect a general attitude about what it means to be secure? How often do you feel deprived or anxious about having enough when in fact your needs are being met?

As you sit down to eat this symbolic meal, pray in thanksgiving for God's providence.

> Therefore I tell you, do not worry about your life, what you will eat [or drink], or about your body, what you will wear. Is not life more than food and the body more than clothing? Look at the birds in the sky; they do not sow or reap, they gather nothing into barns, yet your heavenly Father feeds them. Are you not more important than they? Can any of you by worrying add a single moment to your life-span? (Mt 6:25–27)

## Tuesday: Avoid Looking at Advertisements Today

*The demons wage a veritable war against our concupiscible appetite. They employ for this combat phantasms (and we run to see them) which show conversations*

*with our friends, banquets with our relatives, whole*
*choruses of women and all kinds of other things cal-*
*culated to produce delight. Under the influence of this*
*part of our soul we then grow unhealthy while our*
*passions undergo a full-bodied development.*[3]

### MEDITATION

When Mike and I married nearly three decades ago, our wealth was made up entirely of children, four of them under the age of eight. As a new stepfamily, we had our work cut out for us. Their response to our fledgling marriage ranged from dubious to downright hostile. We could not afford to fan the emotional flames in any way, which led to our first unpopular decision as new stepparents: getting rid of the TV.

Our reasoning went this way: TV offered a steady diet of over-stimulation we couldn't afford, not just through the sensationalized stories it presented but also through its constant barrage of advertising. The ads created desire in the kids for things we either didn't have the money to buy or didn't think were good for them. Even if we'd been wealthy and could give them whatever they wanted, we knew we'd soon regret it; they'd just have more to tussle over.

So, amid indignant shrieks, we carted off the TV and did not look back for many years—long enough for them to get to the so-called age of reason. And even then, it was only when they entered college that they could see the wisdom in this deprivation we'd imposed on them: they told us they were able to focus on their work, to study and learn, in a way that most of their TV-addicted dorm-mates could not.

The desert dwellers' original impetus to flee civilization for the uninhabited wastelands rose out of the same insight: it is far easier to focus on what is good, true, and beautiful when we are not being constantly distracted by temptations toward overeating, over-shopping, and escapist forms of recreation. Though the rampant consumerism of our time was still more than 1,500 years away when the Desert Father movement began, the great cities of the ancient Middle East were filled to overflowing with rich foods and wines, exotic spices and perfumes, gold and jewels, flamboyant silks, and a thousand other temptations toward gluttony, lust, avarice, and envy.

And that combination, the Desert Fathers knew, quickly leads toward chronic sadness arising from disappointed expectations, or to covetousness and the violent anger that can spring up when strong desires are thwarted. As one monk put it, "I have this reason for putting aside pleasure—that I might cut off the pretext for growing angry. For I know that anger constantly fights for pleasure and clouds the mind with passion that drives away contemplative knowledge."[4] Thus, the desert dwellers chose to live in utter poverty and simplicity. Their goal was *apatheia*, or purity of heart, which was a permanent state of freedom from the tyranny of the emotions.

Though we could not shield our kids completely, it's clear that they developed a healthy skepticism toward advertising that has carried over into adulthood. And that was our goal: by getting rid of the TV, we hoped that, like the desert dwellers, they would be able to resist the pressure to mindlessly consume what they didn't need, to covet what they couldn't afford, or to go into debt for the sake of fleeting and distracting pleasures.

## PRACTICE

Today, consciously avoid looking at or listening to any advertising, whether it be on the Internet, in magazines, on the radio, or on TV. The easiest way to do this is to keep all these devices turned off, but if you have to use one of them, pray first for the ability to recognize, then avoid, any ads that pop up. Pray also for insight into your own susceptibility to constant advertising. Are you ever overwhelmed by the urge to go shopping? Do you find it comforting to spend money, even money you don't have? Do you find yourself judging your own appearance on the basis of people you see in ads?

> No servant can serve two masters. He will either hate one and love the other, or be devoted to one and despise the other. You cannot serve God and mammon. . . . What is of human esteem is an abomination in the sight of God. (Lk 16:13, 15)

## Wednesday: Today, Walk to the Store Instead of Driving

*Abbot Pastor said: Just as bees are driven out by smoke, and their honey is taken away from them, so a life of ease drives out the fear of the Lord from man's soul and takes away all his good works.*[5]

### MEDITATION

Some years after we got married, I was awarded a writer's travel grant that allowed us to take the family to Europe. But even a very generous grant could not cover six people traveling in style. So we compromised; we'd rent a small van, we'd haul tents, we'd sleep in campgrounds every night, and we'd do all our own cooking. This way, we could stretch a week's worth of wandering into five.

By the time we landed in Amsterdam, we'd added our former Dutch exchange student and my recently widowed mom to the passenger list, so every seat in our eight-passenger van was filled. Since the majority of the crew were teenagers, pulling together our daily food supplies was a top priority. Each morning after breakfast, we'd hike from the campground to a bakery, a farmer's market, and a grocery store and buy everything we needed for the next twenty-four hours. Though our menus were simple—baguettes, cheese, fruit, milk, couscous, and veggies, plus an evening chocolate bar, split between us—it took some effort to find all the ingredients, and we soon learned to stick with the essentials.

One evening we set up camp in the shadow of a great ruined castle on a hill, a perfect spot for sunset watching, though everybody was too footsore to appreciate it. I also seemed to be the only one who cared about dinner: my teenaged helpers had melted away to their tents, Mike was studying the map, and my mom was writing in her journal. I couldn't really blame them; I knew they were all famished, but even I wasn't particularly thrilled by yet another one-pot meal.

Then my head went up, and my nose began to quiver. Before I could even think about it, I was grabbing my backpack and heading back down the hill to town, a good half mile at least. But if I were right . . . I was! Golden brown, running with juices, a plump hen, squeezed in among her many sisters, was just making a final turn on the street-side rotisserie when I arrived. I handed over some money, the proprietor plucked the bird from the spit and wrapped her up in layers of paper, and back I went up that long hill with a succulent roasted fowl cradled in my arms. The moment my exhausted family caught the scent, they came back to life; that meal, consumed with fervent gratitude, was unanimously voted the best of the trip.

People who are otherwise impressed by the holiness of the Desert Fathers and Mothers are often put off by their rigorous, sometimes extreme, lifestyle. Why would anyone choose to live in such a harsh environment where water was almost nonexistent and it was nearly impossible to grow food? Why put their bodies through such unnecessary hardship? Though the answer is complicated, here is at least one good reason: they understood that those of us who live in a society of plenty often miss out on an important experience: the visceral sense of what our easy pleasures cost in actual human terms. What is so readily available more often than not gets taken for granted. When we always have more than enough to eat, the capacity for gratitude at mealtime is thus diminished.

In a beautifully ironic way, the power of ascetical disciplines, meant to loosen the stranglehold of our desires, is not limited to showing us where we are weak and prone to sin. It does not even end at teaching us self-control. By giving us the opportunity to genuinely value what we would otherwise take for granted, asceticism also has the power to enliven authentic gratitude and wonder.

### PRACTICE

The plethora of food available in today's supermarkets, coupled with the fact that most of us own cars, turns the daily chore of food-gathering into a perfunctory task rather than an occasion for thanksgiving. Today, try walking or biking to the store or to a farmer's market instead of driving. Wear a backpack or carry cloth bags, and be sure not to buy

too much this first time on foot, for whatever you do buy
will become an increasingly heavy burden on the way home.

> I am the bread of life; whoever comes to me will
> never hunger, and whoever believes in me will
> never thirst. (Jn 6:35)

## Thursday: Cut Up One Credit Card

*A certain brother asked of an elder, saying: If a brother
owes me a little money, do you think I should ask him
to pay me back? The elder said to him: Ask him for it
once only, and with humility. The brother said: Sup-
pose I ask him once and he doesn't give me anything,
what should I do? Then the elder said: Don't ask him
any more. The brother said again: But what can I
do, I cannot get rid of my anxieties about it, unless
I go and ask him? The elder said to him: Forget your
anxieties. The important thing is not to sadden your
brother, for you are a monk.*[6]

### MEDITATION

I received another writing grant a few years after I received my first, and this one came with leave from my university teaching job. The amount of money offered was not

enormous, but it was generous enough that, with some planning and frugality, I could stretch it into a round-the-world plane ticket. Soon I had a two-month, seven-country itinerary planned. I also had a terrible case of anxiety, for this time, I would be traveling all on my own.

Some of my worries were justified. On the second day of the trip, a pickpocket on a Greek train got into my backpack and stole my camera. I was robbed again in Jerusalem of several hundred shekels I couldn't really spare. Some gypsy children tried their best to relieve me of my backpack in Ukraine. A Russian tricked me into giving him a handout far larger than I meant to give. When I tried to withdraw money from an ATM in Kazakhstan, nothing came out: the machine was so new, the employees didn't realize you needed to fill it first. By the time I got to India, I was worn out with worry: how could I get my hands on more cash in places that didn't take credit cards?

Without yet being sure what to do, I went ahead and hired a driver who was soon taking me to fascinating places not on the usual tourist route. One of these was an ancient fort in the heart of an enormous city. We arrived at the gate in the midst of a jostling crowd, and instinctively I clutched my purse, edging sideways through the sea of people and praying not to be robbed again. Then I felt the driver's hand on my arm. "Madame," he said, "there is no need."

"What do you mean?"

"For that." He gestured toward the football hold I had on my bag.

Suddenly I could see what I must look like to him: an anxious American who wanted to see India but was so focused on her money she couldn't even enjoy it. "You don't think I need to worry?" I asked a bit self-defensively.

"Madame," he said quietly, "it's a free life."

The goal of the desert dwellers was freedom from anxiety over worldly concerns; one method of achieving this was a radical renunciation of artificial security, particularly hoarded savings. The Rule of St. Benedict, based in part on the experiences of the desert dwellers, zeroes in on the fact that we cannot give ourselves entirely to God if we continue to obsess about having enough. Thomas Merton explains that letting go of our demands for total security is not easy, but when we do, the result is liberation on a grand scale. "The purpose of monastic detachment," he says, "is simply to leave the monk unencumbered, free to move, in possession of his spiritual senses and of his right mind, capable of living a charismatic life in freedom of spirit."[7]

### PRACTICE

Most of us have felt the pinch of not having enough money at times, but our society makes it easy to go into debt when we run low. Credit cards can give us a false sense of security when it might be better to rely on God's loving care. Today, cut up one card as a symbolic blow for freedom from unnecessary anxiety about money.

> But seek first the kingdom [of God] and his righteousness, and all these things will be given you besides. (Mt 6:33)

## Friday: Create a Budget

*"Obedience, together with temperance, brings even wild beasts into subjection," said Anthony the Great.*[8]

### MEDITATION

Before we started building our retirement house, we had to cut down some trees to widen the site. When we finally moved in, things looked pretty bare. Then an adult education catalog arrived in the mail, offering a course in landscape design. I signed up. Maybe, I thought, I can learn enough to come up with a real landscaping plan.

Landscape design turned out to be a lot more involved than I expected. I discovered that I couldn't just eyeball our property and plunk a shrub here and a tree there and wind up with a unified picture. During the sixteen-week course, we studied styles, forms, color, and texture, and it wasn't until the end of the quarter that we were finally ready to talk about plant selection. First, however, our teacher passed out a preliminary maintenance questionnaire. "To come up with a good landscape plan," he told us, "you've got to start by figuring out how much time and energy you're spending on the property as it currently exists. If your goal is to have a sustainable landscape, one that doesn't require hours of labor every day, then you need to recognize where you are already overextended."

The list of questions covered every aspect of our property, and the answers were weighted numerically. Did we have a drainage problem? Add three points. Did we have areas of deep shade or unrelenting sun? Add two more. Did we have slopes, clay soil, rose gardens, vegetables, fruit trees, ponds, or pastures to contend with? Add many, many points. And finally, did we have any of the following red-flag trees, the ones that succumbed to every disease that came down the pike? Glumly, I totaled up the damage; we had them all.

Then our teacher asked everyone for their scores, which he recorded on the black board in columns marked "low," "medium," and "high maintenance." The higher the score, the higher the daily workload. Most people came in somewhere in the mid-thirties, signaling a serious but still reasonable gardening chore list. A few lucky souls had scores in the teens—those with, no doubt, lots of gravel and a few random succulents. Several others admitted they were pushing the envelope, with scores as high as the mid-forties. Then the spotlight was on me.

"We have a really big place," I began apologetically. "Almost four acres."

"And?"

"And so my score's pretty high. It's—would you believe it?—121."

Everyone chuckled, then quieted down when they realized I wasn't joking. Our teacher looked at me for many seconds, then turned to the chalkboard and added a new column: "Completely Unrealistic."

This was an embarrassing moment but also revelatory. For years, Mike and I had been slowly losing steam as we struggled to maintain our place. And now, for the first time, I could see why. The questionnaire had given me incontrovertible evidence that, when it came to gardening, our eyes had always been bigger than our stomachs. No matter how much we loved our forty-tree fruit orchard, our quarter acre of raised-bed vegetables, our roses, our cut flowers, our olive trees, our bee hives, and our turtle pond—all of which required hours of manual labor every single day—we were ridiculously overextended. Two people alone—especially people who were not exactly young anymore—simply could not keep up. It was time to make an honest assessment about what to keep and what to let go. Any future gardening projects had to fit within a realistic "energy budget."

The desert dwellers understood how difficult it is to acknowledge the full ramifications of our impulsive acts. Their remedy, manifestation of one's thoughts to an elder, prevented young and inexperienced monks from blindly following their own noses. As Amma Syncletia put it, "We who have chosen this way of life must obtain perfect temperance." And more, "At all times a lack of moderation is destructive."[9]

A loving spiritual father or mother can become the guide who saves us from succumbing to our most scatterbrained impulses, but holy advisors can be hard to come by in this day and age. Sometimes, we simply need to talk with someone like my landscape design teacher, whose years of hands-on experience gave him the ability to show me what I desperately needed to learn. In the absence of a good guide, we can at least try to rein in our impulsive behavior by realistically budgeting our time, energy, or money.

### PRACTICE

An intemperate lifestyle, which uses up resources we do not have, is not sustainable and ultimately leads to some form of interior disintegration. Today, pray for clarity of vision in regard to your particular form of blind enthusiasm and the unnecessary stress it may be causing in your life. Then sit down and draw up a budget that might help guide you through a restructuring process in this area.

> Come to me, all you who labor and are burdened,
> and I will give you rest. (Mt 11:28)

## Saturday: Give to a Charity

*A certain brother, renouncing the world, and giving the things he owned to the poor, kept a few things in his own possession. He came to Abbot Anthony. When the elder heard about all this, he said to him: If you want to be a monk, go to that village and buy meat, and place it on your naked body and so return here. And when the brother had done as he was told, dogs and birds of prey tore at his body. When he returned to the elder, the latter asked if he had done as he was told. The brother showed him his lacerated body. Then Abbot Anthony said: Those who renounce the world and want to retain possession of money are assailed and torn apart by devils just as you are.*[10]

### MEDITATION

Our town is filled with people who get involved. One couple has turned their private residence into a public meeting hall, funding agricultural experts from around the world to come speak about sustainable farming methods. There, I heard about an organization that teaches subsistence farmers in impoverished countries how to increase production without having to purchase any expensive tools, fertilizers, or seed. Impressed, I signed us up as donors.

What I didn't realize when I joined was that this admirable organization was so committed to sending the bulk of their contributions overseas that they relied upon donors like me to minimize the cost of their stateside operation. When staff members went on the road to raise funds, we were asked to feed and house them. To the staff, donors represented more than dollar signs; we were their community. I understood the rationale and respected the concept, but this was a very busy time in my life and I really didn't have the freedom to participate at this level; somewhat guiltily, I wished they'd just take our monthly checks and leave us alone.

But no. First, we housed the regional director for a night, then we put up the president of the organization, and later, we lodged one of the board members. These were impressive people, and we thoroughly enjoyed our time with them, but still! We had so much else going; it didn't seem fair that we kept getting called on to help out. Weren't we already giving enough?

Then Hurricane Mitch struck Honduras, one of the most devastating storms on record. We knew our organization had been active there for many years and was probably on the scene. Sure enough, several weeks later we got a call from headquarters. "We need housing for our Director of International Affairs. He'll be flying directly from Honduras to your area, filling people in on the situation there, then heading on to Los Angeles. Can you do it?"

How could I object? The next day, an exhausted-looking young man arrived with a single bag and a laptop. He'd spent the past three weeks crisscrossing the devastated countryside by helicopter. Rain-saturated mountainsides had slid down into the valleys, covering some villages with up to nine feet of mud. Farmers had lost their fields, their houses, and their shovels and hoes. Now he was back in the States, hoping to round up tool and seed donations so people could begin growing food before famine set in.

I soon found out that he had a family: a wife, and three small children. He was not going to be able to see them again until the worst of the emergency had been dealt with. Right now, his first priority was checking international e-mail. He turned on his computer and gave me a wry smile. "Over a hundred messages," he said. "Offers of government aid. Volunteers willing to help rebuild. Private donors. And we're not even officially a relief organization." He ran a hand over his tired eyes. "It's really very beautiful," he said.

When I was preparing to become a Camaldolese Benedictine oblate, one of the books I read was about the rebirth of Desert Father spirituality in Italy a thousand years ago. The charism for this new order of "reasonable hermits who live under a rule" was threefold: golden silence, martyrdom, and the privilege of love.[11] A modern prior general, Benedict Calati, often stressed the central place love must take in the life of a monk: "Only a monasticism shaped through and through with love, singing of love, is credible. I . . . [exhort] you all to love one another."[12]

The ancient Christian practice of almsgiving, or making a charitable donation of money to the poor, has its foundation in the same principle. Jesus commands us to "love one another as I have loved you," and watching that weary young man working on into the night, doing his best to mitigate the disastrous effects of a terrible hurricane, showed me what this kind of love looks like in real life. When it comes to charity, money is never enough; God requires our hearts besides.

### PRACTICE

Today, spend some time in prayer on the subject of almsgiving. Perhaps you are already making generous donations to one or more organizations. If so, think about what you might do to help out in a different way, perhaps through volunteer work. If not, search your heart in order to find out what kind of human need or suffering moves you most deeply. This may be a key to what you are being called to give.

> Amen, I say to you, this poor widow put in more than all the other contributors to the treasury. For they have all contributed from their surplus wealth, but she, from her poverty, has contributed all she had, her whole livelihood. (Mk 12:43–44)

# second week of lent:
## SIMPLIFYING THE CARE
## OF THE BODY

The desert dwellers were famously tough on their bodies because they understood that a willingness to undergo discomfort and suffering was a prerequisite for taking up their cross and following Christ.

## Monday: Cover Your Mirrors for a Whole Morning

*Abba Sisoes, the Theban, said to his disciple, "Tell me what you see in me and then I will tell you what I see in you." His disciple said to him, "You are a good man, but a little hard." The old man said to him, "You are good, too, but you are not tough enough."*[1]

### MEDITATION

When the monks have a big project to tackle, one they can't handle on their own, they often call on oblates or other friends of the monastery to help out. A number of years ago, it became apparent that one of their older buildings, an eight-sided chapel, was in dire condition and overdue for a major renovation. Naturally, they thought of Mike. He quickly assembled a team of skilled buddies—men who knew how to swing a hammer, install plumbing, and rewire old buildings—and off they went. An already tricky project was made trickier by the fact that the monastery is at least an hour's winding drive along one-thousand-foot Big Sur cliffs from the nearest hardware store or lumberyard.

But on they hammered, and a month or so later, they were done: the former chapel had been transformed into private guest quarters for visiting religious or the relatives of monks. Mike said goodbye to the team, and he and I spent several more days putting in the finishing touches, which included two large mirrors, designed and beautifully framed in oak by my weary but still idealistic husband. "This one will pick up the light from those high windows," he explained as I steadied it and he drilled in the screws. The other, which took up a third of the wall in the bathroom, would "double the size of the room," he assured me.

When it was finally time to give the monks their first tour of the new guest quarters, I stood back proudly and waited for someone to notice the way the first mirror picked up the window's-eye view of the mountaintop and reflected it back into the room. Everyone was complimentary and full of thanks, but nobody mentioned the mirror.

Then people crowded into the small bathroom, admiring the shower, the wood trim, and even the towel racks, but leaving out entirely any comment about the huge oak-framed expanse of glass above the sink. However, when the visit was over and we were saying goodbye at the door, an oblate who happened to be working that weekend leaned in and said, "Really big mirrors. I mean, really, really big."

I was a little taken aback. "Don't you think they're nice?"

"Sure. In a hotel, maybe. But monks don't do mirrors—remember?"

And now that he'd mentioned it, of course I did. Though the total medieval ban on mirrors for monks has been lifted in many modern monasteries, including at the hermitage, the logic behind it remained: catching glimpses of our own faces whenever we pass through a room cannot, in the long run, be good for us. Each time we peer into the mirror, our minds are set to wondering: Am I looking older these days? Am I as attractive as I used to be? Should I get surgery? Maybe I should get contacts, buy wrinkle cream, or color my hair. Mirrors, by their very nature, focus us on our physical appearance in the most superficial of ways. And by constantly rerouting our thoughts back to how we look, they make us sitting ducks for advertising ploys that promise to make us more attractive.

The traditional monastic ban on mirrors emerged out of a larger context having to do with modesty and the "custody of the eyes." Though we moderns have been convinced that we are immune to the power of what we see and hear, no matter how stimulating, ancient monastic wisdom insisted that everything we experience, even the aftereffect of a lingering glance at a beautiful body, has the ability to shift us onto unsteady spiritual ground.

The solution is to avoid looking at what might lead to lascivious thoughts or erotic dreams—or, for that matter, to a gluttonous appetite, the temptation to drink, greed, envy, or a violent desire for revenge. As the Rule of St. Augustine puts it, "The immodest eye is the messenger of the impure heart."[2]

The most important reason for refusing to stare in bold judgment at someone else or even at our own face in the mirror is that, by so doing, we fail to revere the God-given personhood of each and every human being. We deny the mystery that abides in our depths; we assume we can know, by looking critically and hard, who is worth something and who is not. And in so doing, we are unable to "see" one another, or ourselves, at all.

As for Mike's beautiful mirrors on the walls of the former chapel, they were quietly allowed to stay. I think it was probably the way they caught the light from those high windows.

### PRACTICE

This morning, try your best to practice custody of the eyes when it comes to the mirror. It will be hard to comb your hair, wash your face, and brush your teeth without your own reflection to guide you, but since you do the same things every day, it's likely that gazing into the mirror is simply a habit. As you move through the house, think about how often you glance into the mirror to see if you pass muster. Think also about the harsh judgments you've made about your own appearance over the years, along with the occasional vainglorious "highs" of believing you've never looked so good. Pray to move beyond surface appearances, both with yourselves and with others, and into a state of true seeing.

> The lamp of the body is the eye. If your eye is sound, your whole body will be filled with light; but if your eye is bad, your whole body will be in darkness. (Mt 6:22–23)

## Tuesday: Skip Today's Shower or Bath

*[Abba Poeman] also said, "If a monk can overcome two things, he can become free from the world." The brother asked him what these two things were and he said, "Bodily ease and vainglory."*[3]

### MEDITATION

Every fall, my siblings and I spend a week backpacking in the Sierras with our spouses and a few hardy friends. Even though we always have a wonderful time, the day before we pack up and head for the mountains is marked by dread. What makes me shudder? Not concern about the exertion ahead, nor even fear of getting hurt, but something far more basic: for a whole seven days, we will be miles from the nearest bathroom.

Surprisingly, it is not the lack of a toilet that gets me down. Like the other backpackers on the trail, we each carry an orange plastic trowel and a mini roll of bio-degradable paper. We make jokes about "going troweling" yet discretely preserve one another's privacy by noticing which direction someone has headed and maintaining a wide berth.

No, the pre-hike dread I feel has nothing to do with being deprived of a toilet. It has to do with giving up my nightly soak in the bathtub. One cannot take a proper bath on the trail. On our best days, we'll find ourselves next to a crystalline lake, the temperature will be in the eighties, and we'll have gotten in our daily mileage early enough that we can go for a glacial swim, and then dry off in a warm meadow thick with wildflowers and fluttering butterflies.

But usually, we are not that fortunate. Most afternoons, we pull in an hour and a half later than planned, footsore, sweaty, filthy, and beat. By the time we set up camp, dusk is upon us, and the moment the sun begins to sink, the temperature drops precipitously. So we scurry around collecting our drip-dry camp towels, camp suds, and a couple of gallon-sized plastic food storage bags (washing machines for our underwear), and then troop gingerly off to the nearest stream. There, we make our freezing ablutions behind individual boulders, taking care not to contaminate the pristine water with any suds.

Why do we put ourselves through this cold and complicated ritual when we are so tired and hungry? On the trail, keeping reasonably clean is a safety precaution; it helps prevent infections and provides an opportunity to check for new blisters, ticks, bites, and cuts. Perhaps it also helps preserve good mental health, though when I'm in the midst of one of those rushed arctic scrub-downs, I can't imagine how.

The desert dwellers spent decades living in hot, dry landscapes with nothing but a cave or wattle hut for shelter. How did they bathe? One of them refers to "throwing a little water over his feet" in order to keep clean.[4] More than that, they do not tell us, and I am left imagining that they washed themselves the way a large percentage of the world's population still does today: rarely, and with a daunting amount of effort. However they managed it, I am sure of one thing: they did not long for it as I do, or mope around because they felt deprived. The whole point of their ascetical practices was to detach from cravings for physical pampering. They learned how to do this through habitual self-denial.

Michael Casey explains the rationale behind their voluntary deprivation:

> Whenever we find genuine monasticism, there is an emphasis on a simple, austere way of life in which normal human desires are but scantily fulfilled. Monks serve as a reminder that a life of ease and pleasure is not the best way to find ultimate fulfillment. In a Christian setting those who practice monastic renunciation point to the existence of a richer and fuller life beyond death in eternity.[5]

### PRACTICE

Today, think about the marvel of indoor plumbing, the blessing of bountiful hot running water from the tap, and the luxury of being able to bathe on a daily basis. Imagine yourself in a society or era in which poverty or circumstances dictate that bathing is a rare and special event. As you go without your shower or bath today, pray for release from habits of self-pampering and for an increase in awareness regarding other people's difficult or trying situations.

> If I, therefore, the master and teacher, have washed your feet, you ought to wash one another's feet. (Jn 13:14)

## Wednesday: Wear Your Oldest Clothes Today

*Abba Isaac said that Abba Pambo used to say, "The monk's garment should be such that he could throw it out of his cell for three days and no-one would take it."*[6]

### MEDITATION

Though I am used to leading intimate retreats, I rarely speak to big groups. Recently, however, I was invited to offer workshops at one of the largest Catholic gatherings in the country. My friends let me know they were impressed—I'd never spoken in such a major venue before—but their admiring remarks only deepened my sense of unease. Clearly, I was in over my head. My jitters got worse when I arrived at the conference and took a peek in my room, which was designed to hold a thousand people.

That night, I had a classic dream, the one in which you walk out on a big empty stage and not only are you blinded by the lights but you realize that you have forgotten your lines. Worse still, you can't even remember what play you are supposed to be in. I woke up sweaty and disoriented, vowing to avoid all large-group presentations in the future, if only I could get through the next day without disaster.

As I headed for my first session, praying for steadiness and a peaceful heart, I happened to glance down at my foot. My boot was splitting apart in a horizontal line across the toes. I was about to stand up before a thousand people with a boot so old it had just given up the ghost. At first I was appalled—why hadn't I noticed how worn it was getting?—and then I began to laugh.

God had just answered my prayer: the only way to get up in front of that gargantuan crowd without succumbing to destructive self-consciousness was to let go of the performance anxiety and open myself in humility to whatever happened next. Truth be told, it was not my finest hour. However, it could have been much worse without the reassuring reminder that, while I am precious in the eyes of God, I am "nobody special" and likely never will be. Why try, I asked myself as I limped offstage, to pretend otherwise?

The simplicity of monastic dress is intended to foster anonymity. When everybody wears the same denim work clothes or white robe, nobody stands out. The community has a better chance to become one when it is impossible to discern social status or wealth by the expensive or fashionable clothes someone is wearing. People can stop worrying about their attire; there are more important things to attend to. The Rule of St. Benedict advises monks to sleep fully clothed so that "they will always be ready to arise without delay when the signal is given; each will hasten to arrive at the Work of God before the others."[7]

In an economy fueled by personal spending, the pressure is on to prove, through the fashionable or expensive clothing we wear, that we are making it financially. Stained and ragged garments are for those who work with their hands, for the poor, or for disconcerting social misfits. One of the saddest results of such thinking is that people who cannot afford to keep up with the current style go deeply into debt in order to maintain the facade that they are doing all right.

In the monastic sense, then, the simplicity of dress is deliberately countercultural; it announces that the life of a monk is going to be different than the norm, especially the norm of buying into the superficial standards foisted upon society for commercial purposes. Yet, we do not have to succumb to such thinking. We, too, can embrace simplicity of dress and, in the process, court anonymity.

#### PRACTICE

Today, wear your oldest and least presentable clothes, no matter what's on the schedule. Notice how people react. Think about what it is like to move about in a consumerist society when you cannot afford to keep up appearances. Pray for awareness regarding your own sense of self-worth when you are not "looking your best." Ask to be freed up from this unnecessary self-preoccupation.

> Notice how the flowers grow. They do not toil or spin. But I tell you, not even Solomon in all his splendor was dressed like one of them. (Lk 12:27)

## Thursday: Fast from Sugar, Alcohol, or Fat for a Day

> *To the extent that you still give attention to the values*
> *of the body, and your mind concerns itself with the*
> *amenities of life, you have not yet seen the place of*
> *prayer. Rather the happiness of this way is still far off.*[8]

### MEDITATION

Several years before the great Japan earthquake and tsunami of 2011, a monster tsunami swept across the Indian
Ocean, ultimately killing 230,000 people in fourteen countries. As news of the disaster broke, a shocked world moved
into action, sending supplies, volunteers, and money. Like
so many others, so did we, mailing our check off to the Red
Cross almost as soon as we heard the news.

But it was not until later that week that I found myself weeping as I stared at a newspaper photo of a beautiful
young Sumatran woman standing dazed in a refugee camp.
According to the caption, she'd lost her entire family, and
you could see by the look in her eyes that she did not know
what to do next. Suddenly, I had an overpowering urge to
help her bear her burden, but how? I lived thousands of
miles away, she was not named in the photo, and even if I
got on a plane and went there, I'd never find her.

Then I remembered the story of the philosopher Simone Weil, a young Jewish woman in Germany during the

buildup toward World War II, who eventually became a great mystic, unbaptized but passionately in love with Christ, and died at thirty-four. From the time she was a small child, she had a remarkable sensitivity toward the suffering of others.

When in 1915, at age six, she heard that entrenched French soldiers on the Western Front had no sugar, she refused to eat it herself. Later, as a brilliant young scholar and teacher, she went to work in a factory in order to share the grinding labor that so many people had no choice about doing. At thirty-three, she collapsed with tuberculosis and malnutrition but refused food and medical treatment out of solidarity with the people of occupied France. Many believe that her early death was prompted by this pattern of severe self-denial for the sake of others.

Holding that Indonesian woman's photo in my hand and thinking about Simone Weil's response to suffering led me to a decision: for as long as it took, I would limit myself to that shattered survivor's one daily meal, a bowlful of rice and lentils. Immediately, I felt joined to her in a way that seemed impossible before. And as each day passed with nothing but lentils and rice, I found myself praying that God would richly bless her in her terrible bereavement.

The fasting was not so hard—I'd done it before in other circumstances—but what derailed me before a week was out was the sameness of the diet. Lentils and rice, rice and lentils: no variation, day after day. Though I knew she would go on eating this way for many months, and though I knew that all over the world people eat this way habitually because they have no other options, I could not stop craving the pleasures of variety. My hungry stomach would make its demands—after fasting all day, I deserve more than lentils and rice! I want grilled salmon and an arugula salad instead! And inevitably I began to cave in.

Hard as it was to fail, the experience helped me face reality. I was no Simone Weil (few of us are), and I'd fallen into the trap of thinking I could emulate a great spiritual exemplar without going through the long discipline and difficult formation it takes to live the way she lived. Rather than cast myself in a romantic role I could not fulfill, it was much healthier, not to mention more honest, to be up front about my weaknesses, including the irresistible urge for grilled salmon. The original idea—fasting in solidarity with someone who was suffering—had not been wrong, however, and the impulse was good: we can indeed participate in the suffering of others if we are prayerfully willing to offer up something of ourselves, no matter how small, for their sakes. If this self-sacrificial urge flows from genuine love, then the offering, no matter how meager, still has the power to in some way bless.

### PRACTICE

Today, forego your usual serving of sugar, alcohol, or fat—whichever is most important to you—in the name of someone else who is too ill or too poor to eat the way you do. Imagine this person's face, and throughout the day, ask God to be near. Give thanks when you feel a pang of regret for what you cannot have today, for this sense of deprivation is the mark of your participation in the suffering of someone else.

> I came down from heaven not to do my own will
> but the will of the one who sent me. (Jn 6:38)

## Friday: Sleep on the Floor for a Night

*An elder said: A man who keeps death before his eyes will at all times overcome his cowardice.*[9]

### MEDITATION

The only time I recall sleeping on the hard floor without any mattress, pillow, or blanket was in a crowded hospital waiting room, surrounded by relatives and friends. My little niece was dying, and we'd come to keep vigil with her parents. At the end of that first long day, it did not seem right to leave, nor did anyone want to, so we got permission from the hospital staff to sleep on whatever sofas and chairs we could find. Those were quickly filled, and some of us wound up on the floor.

It was a long night. Though all of us were emotionally drained, it was difficult to sleep. Through those dark, uncomfortable hours on thin carpeting, I found myself thinking about death—not only the impending death of that beloved child but also the death that I would someday face myself. At this time in my life, I had been away from Christianity for many years. My heart had become hardened against religion, and there was nothing anyone could say that could soften it. People tried, and when they did, I invariably flew into a rage. I told myself that I would not put up with anyone's unwanted advice. I was a free being, answerable to no one.

Yet, here I was, face down on a grainy hospital rug, surrounded by quietly breathing, quietly grieving friends and relatives, most of them people of faith. And suddenly I felt an immense gulf yawning open beneath me. My sister was losing her only child. How would she bear it? I didn't think I could—yet, as a woman of faith, she would not only survive but also eventually be able to place this unfathomable loss into a context of meaning, a rich framework entirely unavailable to me.

The keeping of vigils is an ancient monastic practice. While the rest of the world slept, the old hermits and monks stayed awake, deliberately depriving themselves of sleep to pray through the dark watches of the night for the safety and protection of humankind. For them, the wilderness was the dark abode of Satan and his demons, the kingdom of death. Sometimes, like St. Anthony, they purposely inhabited tombs to put themselves in closer contact with the enemy. They were vigilant warriors whose weapon was prayer.

But they also believed in keeping physical death before their eyes, an inescapable reality for every human being. The contemplation of death, they thought, put everything else into perspective: it highlighted the ephemeral nature of life, it brought into focus the brevity of time, and it infused a sense of urgency into their daily Work of God. St. Benedict believed that a regular practice of remembering death was a great spur toward faithfulness.

The difference between this kind of relationship to death and the one I experienced during the hospital vigil for my niece was lodged in my unbelief. For me at that time, death was nothing but a cold abyss, meaningless and cruel. However, Cistercian Michael Casey offers another view: "Our Christian faith keeps reminding us that death is the doorway to eternal life, so that there is no need to blot it out of consciousness. . . . One of the high points of monastic profession is the triple chant of the Suscipe: 'Receive me, O Christ, according to your promise and I shall live; do not disappoint me of my hope.'"[10]

As people who love deeply, we cannot avoid the suffering of death-caused grief. We can, however, be released from the terrible fear of annihilation that accompanies faithlessness and unbelief. Though this peaceful equanimity in the face of death is difficult to achieve, by adopting an ascetical practice

that helps us confront what we most fear, we prepare ourselves for the moment when we must take our leave.

## PRACTICE

Today, try sleeping on the floor for the first hour of the
night. Think about your own death. Ask God to help you
ponder what is almost impossible to comprehend. Ask him
for wisdom and insight, and most of all, hope in the promises of Christ. Then go off to your warm bed in a state of
thanksgiving.

> Watch, therefore; you do not know when the lord
> of the house is coming, whether in the evening,
> or at midnight, or at cockcrow, or in the morn-
> ing. May he not come suddenly and find you
> sleeping. What I say to you, I say to all: "Watch!"
> (Mk 13:35–37)

## Saturday: Spend Some Time Kneeling in Prayer Today

*Happy the man who thinks himself no better than
dirt.*[11]

### MEDITATION

The first time I saw Christians making prostrations was on a Holy Thursday in Greece. We were visiting an ancient convent on one of the islands, but because it was Lent, prostrations were going on in Orthodox parishes around the world. Standing for long periods, bowing frequently, kneeling on stone-cold floors, and touching one's head to the ground are still common in Eastern Christian worship, as is standing, genuflecting, and kneeling in the Catholic Mass.

I still found the prostrations shocking, however. Aren't such symbolic acts of obeisance degrading? In a modern, secular democracy like ours, they can easily raise the image of peasants groveling before aristocratic overlords—the very tyrants from whom we liberated ourselves nearly two hundred and fifty years ago. As the progeny of Yankee rebels, we are ingrained with the notion that it is wrong to bend the knee to any man. So why continue to genuflect, kneel, and prostrate ourselves before the God who has invited us to stand before him as reconciled sons and daughters?

Yet, as I watched the parishioners in this ancient convent chapel touching their heads to the floor, I felt strangely moved to join them. And suddenly, in this act of bending humbly to the ground, my heart welled up with tears of apology for all the ways in which I had slighted my beloved and merciful Abba during the past year. Not only had I disregarded his most solemn words, but I had rebelliously disobeyed him as well and then pitied myself when the negative results inevitably followed. With my head against the cold stone floor, I could not avoid seeing what I normally refused to look at: my persistent pettiness, my self-centeredness, my inflated sense of importance, and my abysmal ignorance. And this was an awful revelation. In so many ways, I really was nothing but dirt—but also, miraculously, loved beyond measure.

The Rule of St. Benedict prescribes a harsh-sounding punishment for a monk who has been temporarily excommunicated from worship and the table for serious faults. Says Benedict, "He should lie face down at the feet of all as they leave the oratory, and let him do this until the abbot judges he has made satisfaction. Next, at the bidding of the abbot, he is to prostrate himself at the abbot's feet, then at the feet of all that they may pray for him."[12] Esther de Waal explains that this regulation is intended to make sure there is "true repentance, a recognition of what sin does to others and to God, as well as to oneself."[13]

Genuflecting, kneeling, and prostrating are symbols of obedience and acts of reverence to the Most High God. But they are also outward and visible signs of our ever-weak, ever-sinful human condition. They indicate that we recognize, however ruefully, what we would be without Christ— who we would be as naked and unaided human beings. They acknowledge what we so often are, living as we do in a cloud of distractions and forgetfulness.

### PRACTICE

Today, find a place where you can kneel for ten minutes without interruption. You might be able to do this at church, perhaps before the Blessed Sacrament, or at home in front of an icon. During this time, your knees will ache and you will most likely feel tension in your body because of the unfamiliar position you are holding. If you are physically unable to kneel, then find a position that reflects compunction. Try to ignore any physical signs of discomfort and simply focus on quieting your mind. Think of the ways that you have wounded others and failed to revere God. Think about your habitual failures to love. Acknowledge your weakness. Then apologize and ask for forgiveness.

> Blessed are the poor in spirit, for theirs is the kingdom of heaven. (Mt 5:3)

# third week of lent:
## SIMPLIFYING THE MIND

The desert dwellers believed that our souls need proper nourishment—spiritual food—in order to achieve clear spiritual vision. Jesus often withdrew into the desert or the mountaintops at night in order to rejuvenate his soul through prayer.

## Monday: Spend a Day Without TV

*A brother, possessed by sadness and melancholy, went to an Elder and asked of him: "What am I to do? My thoughts present me with the idea that perhaps in vain I denied the world and that I cannot be saved."*

*Thoughtfully, the Elder answered as follows: "My child, even if we do not succeed in reaching the promised land, it is better that we should give our carcasses to the desert than return to the Egypt of fearful enslavement" (Numbers 14:29–33).[1]*

### MEDITATION

I live in a busy place. With a garden, orchard, kitchen, and grandkids to care for, my mornings are filled with physical labor. By the time I sit down for lunch, I'm tired. But then I go to my studio, where I spend the next four or five hours researching and writing. When I get back to the house at six or so, it's time to cook the evening meal, eat dinner, and clean up the kitchen. As the working day draws to a close, I find myself fighting to stay awake. But 8:00 p.m. is just too early to go to bed. Instead, I look around for something that will not only keep me up but also distract me!

All sorts of options exist. From movie channels to cable TV to the Internet, society offers us myriad ways to artificially reinvigorate the mind. And when I am really tired, they are hard to resist. After all, what could be wrong with a little entertainment after a long day's work?

What's wrong is that a steady diet of over-stimulating or fantasy-inducing distraction eventually reshapes our perception of the world and prevents us from dealing with reality. Twenty-five years ago, long before cable channels or stirring websites existed, Neil Postman wrote an analysis of the way that television was reshaping our view of the world. The problem, he said, was not so much that TV was entertaining. Life is hard, and everyone needs a momentary lift on occasion. The problem was that TV had come to dominate the culture, which meant that almost all our experiences were now coming to us as entertainment rather than in the form of serious intellectual, moral, or spiritual questions.

When we watch TV, all we have to do is make a simple, childish choice: is this interesting or boring? If it fails to pass the test, we just flip the channel and move on. It's not surprising that even newscasters have succumbed to the entertainment trend: unless they over-stimulate us or lead us into the escapist fantasies we've come to expect, why would we watch them?

Jesus, however, links genuine freedom to our ability to recognize truth. "If you remain in my word, you will truly be my disciples, and you will know the truth, and the truth will set you free" (Jn 8:31–32). Free from what? Misperception, melodrama, falsehood, artificiality, superficiality, and self-indulgent egoism—everything the entertainment industry depends upon to hold our attention.

One evening it occurred to me that turning to entertainment for stimulation and distraction when I was mentally exhausted was like drinking caffeine when what I really needed was a good nap. Was there any reason I couldn't give my tired mind a rest instead of artificially invigorating it?

I put on my down jacket and slipped out onto the front porch, my morning place of prayer. The sky was velvet black and spangled with bright stars. A great horned owl was hooting throatily nearby, and his lady love was answering: a cello duet among the trees. I sat for a long time—nearly an hour—and slowly felt my mind withdraw from the concerns of the day, from the knotty, unsolved writing problems I'd left behind in the studio, and from worry and stress. I felt alert but peaceful—no longer in danger of falling asleep. Moreover, I felt blessedly clear and clean: free as the cold night air.

### PRACTICE

Today, fast from TV. If you are not a TV watcher, then choose another form of entertainment that you rely upon to keep you stimulated and distracted. Notice what happens when this habitual method of reinvigorating yourself is removed. Do you feel restless? Bored? How deeply ingrained is the entertainment addiction? While you fast, pray for new insight in this area and for the strength to try new ways of dealing with mental exhaustion.

> I am the light of the world. Whoever follows me will not walk in darkness, but will have the light of life. (Jn 8:12)

## Tuesday: Spend a Day Without E-mail, Facebook, and Other Social Networking Tools

*A certain brother came, once, to Abbot Theodore of Pherme, and spent three days begging him to let him*

*hear a word. The Abbot however did not answer him,
and he went off sad. So a disciple said to Abbot Theodore: Father, why did you not speak to him? Now he
has gone off sad! The elder replied: Believe me, I spoke
no word to him because he is a trader in words and
seeks to glory in the words of another.*[2]

## MEDITATION

After nearly twenty years of calling myself an atheist,
something began to shift inside. I became aware of a deep
and urgent hunger I'd not experienced before. I realized I
was assessing people in a new way, wondering if they believed in God and, if so, why. Though at first these strange
and intrusive thoughts were a bit scary—after all, much of
my identity was tied up in my supposed atheism—I could
not seem to shake off a growing thirst for spiritual conversation. Yet, by now, I was going through graduate school on a
big, secular campus where most people seemed to think that
faith was impossible among the intelligent and well edu-
cated. Who could I talk to about these unlikely stirrings?

Eventually, I found a mentor, an ethics professor who
was willing to deal with the many questions I'd put on the
back burner when I gave up on religion. As long as my que-
ries were intellectual ones, he was perfectly forthcoming.
He'd call me on my logic, point out where I'd mixed up the
facts, and fill in missing gaps for me. In time, all my intellectual defenses against Christianity had been leveled, and

suddenly I was moving into a new stage: re-conversion to the religion of my childhood.

In this new place, murky and obscure, I stumbled along, terrified and suspicious but already resigned to the fact that I was going to succumb to God's promptings at some point. Again, my spiritual teacher was extremely helpful, suggesting books I might read, introducing me to his Catholic wife, and pointing me toward the hermitage for the first time. Eventually, I caved in and, with fearful jubilation, rededicated myself to a life of following Christ.

Filled with new zeal, I could hardly wait to share my exciting new experiences with my guide. I flooded him with requests for more information, I babbled on and on about how much I was learning, and soon I found myself advising others as confused as I had been. Strangely, however, when I got to this stage, he suddenly went silent—not completely but noticeably.

At first I was puzzled, then hurt. What had gone wrong? Was it something I said? Finally, I got up the courage to ask him why he was so quiet these days. He wouldn't say—but he suggested, obliquely, that I might think about being quieter myself, that listening, rather than talking, might be a wiser way to proceed at this point.

It took a long time for me to figure it out, though finally I did: he had seen that beneath my honest joy and zeal lay the shadow of unconquered vainglory. Before my humbling re-conversion, I was used to being seen as someone special.

I was a diligent student, a published writer, and a person of substance. Jesus had now leveled me, and I couldn't rely on those old ways of measuring status anymore. However, I could counsel others about how to find him, just as my mentor had counseled me. What I failed to see was that I was still completely wet behind the ears; trying to take on the role of spiritual guide for others before I was ready was imprudent, especially for someone still struggling with the need to be important.

No wonder he had gone silent on me. He'd seen the potential danger in what I was up to—I might be tempted to pass on knowledge I didn't actually have or rely on my verbal skill, rather than genuine spiritual insight, to persuade people of something I didn't yet understand myself. However innocently, I might be treating holy words as though they were commodities, meant to enhance my own status, rather than with the reverence they deserved.

A fourth-century monk of Palestine, John Cassian, got permission to go to the Egyptian desert in search of the great spiritual elders. He and his friend Germanus ultimately spent fifteen years moving from skete to monastery, talking with the Fathers of the desert. He watched how they handled the many eager pilgrims who sought them out, begging for a "word to live by."

The elders never gave that word unless they were first sure of the seeker's intentions. Was this another curiosity seeker who would return to the big city and tell his tall tales to public applause? Was this a neophyte believer who was not yet ready to handle real spiritual food? Would they be throwing their pearls before swine, as scripture warned them not to do?

If the seeker passed muster, a word might (or might not) be forthcoming; only God could give that treasure via his faithful servant. If God did not choose to speak, then neither did the elder. For they knew that words are full of grace and have the power to charge the world with holiness. Like my concerned mentor, they knew that we squander them at our peril.

### PRACTICE

We live in a time of incredibly easy access to words. We can instantly communicate with hundreds of friends and relatives simply by touching a few keys. We can speak to one another with lightning speed and almost without thought. Today, in honor of the holiness of words, stay away from e-mail, Facebook, and all other social networking sites. Allow silence to take the place of electronic chatter for a while. Notice what you are thinking about when you are not thinking about connecting with or checking up on people. Instead, pray for them.

> If you remain in me and my words remain in you,
> ask for whatever you want and it will be done for
> you. (Jn 15:7)

## Wednesday: Turn Off Your Cell Phone for a Day

*A great thing indeed—to pray without distraction; a greater thing still—to sing psalms without distraction.*[3]

### MEDITATION

New visitors to the hermitage notice right away that there is no cell phone coverage. Not only that, but the landline is unpredictable. Most of the time it works fine, but on other occasions—usually in the midst of a big storm—it fails completely. Since storms that size often cause landslides that block the one road in and out, the hermitage can easily become disconnected from the world.

We modern types are not used to being cut adrift in this way. We are used to having 911 at our fingertips, not to mention a platoon of emergency vehicles speeding toward us if we should call for help. True isolation stirs the demons of anxiety.

Years ago, when I was still thinking about becoming an oblate, I headed for the hermitage for a couple of nights. As I got on the highway heading north, I could see some ominous thunderclouds up ahead, so I called the bookstore office to ask about the weather: no response; the landline must be out again. A bit uneasy—potential danger!—I kept driving.

Once I arrived, everything seemed normal, despite the lowering skies—everything, that is, but the water supply.

Somewhere on the mountainside a water line had snapped, and even though they'd been busily digging for several days, they hadn't yet been able to solve the problem. I learned this from the young monk who showed up at my guesthouse door with a big water tank in the back of the monastery pick-up. "Should be soon," he said, as I filled up my pitcher.

Later, I took my usual evening walk with an old friend, a exuberant French-Canadian monk called Fr. Bernard, and as we walked down the mountain, we kept stopping to *oooh* and *aaah* about the spectacular lightning show going on over the ocean. We both agreed we'd never seen one like it before; it looked as though it might be threatening a couple of hundred miles of coastline. The greatest danger in the Big Sur wilderness, aside from a major earthquake, is dry lightning, which frequently sets off forest fires in inaccessible areas.

During the night, I was jarred awake by a bolt so close that I thought my trailer had been struck. Outside, the wind was howling, but I couldn't hear rain: not good. I thought about getting up to look but hesitated to step out into the storm. By the time the bell for Lauds rang the next morning, the air was thick with ashy smoke and it looked as though there were at least three separate fires burning: one to the north and two to the south.

My first impulse was to grab the cell phone and call Mike, but then I remembered: no cell phone coverage— also, no water and no landline. What were we going to do? I threw on my clothes and trotted up to the chapel, assuming we'd be forgoing the prayer service for an emergency planning session.

Not so. The monks were gathered as usual, two rows of silent, white-robed men with heads calmly bowed in meditation. We proceeded with the morning psalms, the readings, and the prayers of the faithful. Then we were done, and nobody had yet leaped to his feet to bark out emergency orders. I began to fidget; shouldn't we be doing something?

As the monks filed out, the prior stepped aside and waited until they were gone. Then he spoke to the few of us sitting hopefully in the pews. A fire crew had already been up to check on things. The advice was that we should pack up and drive out while we still could. Though we'd be passing through smoky areas, the fires were still high up enough on the ridge that we should be fine. "But what about all of you?" we asked him. "What are you going to do?" He smiled and told us not to worry; they'd been through this before, and they'd evacuate if need be. The bigger issue was making sure we were safely on the road before too long.

Tranquility in the face of danger speaks to purity of heart. The God-centered soul is calm in a way the self-centered soul can never be. Years of prayerful self-discipline truly manifest their efficacy when catastrophe strikes. Like wildflower seeds that do not sprout until they have been razed in forest fires, the virtues instilled by the contemplative life come into their own when everyone else is fleeing for their lives.

**PRACTICE**

Cell phones connect us to the world—particularly now, when they can connect us to the Internet as well. With a cell phone in our pocket, we feel somehow invulnerable; there will always be someone to distract us, rescue us, reassure us, or simply cheer us up. Unless we make a point of not doing so, it's easy to rely on cell phones more than we rely on God.

Today, turn off your cell and enter your day undefended. Every time you are tempted to get in touch with someone via the phone, pray instead.

> While you have the light, believe in the light, so that
> you may become children of the light. (Jn 12:36)

## Thursday: Spend Fifteen Minutes in Silence Today

*A certain brother went to Abbot Moses in Scete and asked him for a good word. And the elder said to him: Go, sit in your cell, and your cell will teach you everything.*[4]

**MEDITATION**

Some years ago, I went to Italy with a group of monks and oblates to visit the ancient houses of the thousand-year-old

Camaldolese order. At one hermitage high in the mountains, I found a meditation chapel shaped like the belly of Jonah's whale, with whitewashed ribs and stone flesh. The tiny chapel was filled with high-backed wooden benches, so private it was impossible to see who was kneeling there. I slipped into one of them, knelt, and closed my eyes. This was not a time for making petitions or offering up gratitude and praise: instead, this was entirely about silence.

The Camaldolese are a contemplative order, which means they devote a goodly portion of each day to *quies* (rest) and *hesychia* (sweet repose)—in other words, to sitting in silence in their cells, in the unlit rotunda of the church, or out in nature. Their founder, Romuald of Ravenna, says in his Brief Rule, "Sit in your cell as in a paradise. Put the whole world behind you and forget it. Watch your thoughts like a good fisherman watching for fish. . . . Empty yourself completely and sit waiting, content with the grace of God, like the chick who tastes nothing and eats nothing but what his mother brings him."[5] Romuald wrote his Rule nearly seven hundred years after the Desert Father phenomenon, but his emphasis on silence, stillness, and patient waiting is classic desert spirituality.

What does silence accomplish in us? According to the desert dwellers, the Camaldolese, and other contemplative orders, it accomplishes everything. The discipline of sitting in silence slowly calms our bodily urge to be up and doing something "useful." It swings our spiritual gyroscope back to home point. It teaches us to recollect our anxious minds, to surrender our need for absolute control, and to expand our narrow vision. Most of all, however, it leads to the primary monastic virtue of love.

For a long time, including that day in the high-mountain hermitage in Italy, I could not see how silence led to love. If anything, the disciplined practice of silence seemed to sever me from other people, to hyper-sensitize me to their noisy chatter, and to increase my longing for withdrawal from the world. I did not feel particularly loving toward my fellow human beings; in fact, with their unrelenting demands for time and attention, they were more like obstacles than love objects.

Then I heard a story from one of the monks, who had been in Biafra during the great famine of the 1960s. He said that, when he visited the refugee camps, he learned something very interesting: people who are starving cannot handle food; their systems have adjusted themselves in expectation of dying. They must be fed spoonfuls of juice, a sip at a time, for an extended period before they can take in anything solid. He added, "I began to think about the spiritual starvation in our world today—how people in this state can only handle the gentlest spoon-feeding of religion or their psyches will automatically reject it."

And there was the key: silence as practiced by the hermits and monks of ancient Christianity was meant to teach humility and all of its attendant virtues: focused listening, compassion, patience, gentleness, and loving-kindness.

People who are comfortable with silence have had to let go of numerous impediments along the way: by the time they close their eyes in a darkened rotunda or slip into a high-backed pew in the stone belly of a stone whale, they understand that silence in the presence of God renews and refreshes their spirits—and gives them the ability to give generously in return.

As Fr. Daniel pointed out in his Biafra story, only in the hands of those who've mastered the art of silence is the Gospel truly safe from abuse at the hands of the self-righteous. It is the Hesychast—the silent one—who can offer it to parched souls gently enough for it to be accepted.

### PRACTICE

Several weeks ago, you established a private area for prayer. Go to that area today and sit for fifteen minutes in total silence. Do not think about your problems, your to-do list, your friends and family who are in need, or the dire circumstances of the world. Do not even think about God. Simply sit waiting, like an obedient chick, for whatever its mother might offer next.

> Let the children come to me and do not prevent them; for the kingdom of God belongs to such as these. Amen, I say to you, whoever does not accept the kingdom of God like a child will not enter it. (Lk 18:16–17)

## Friday: Read About How to Do Lectio Divina, and Then Try It

> *The effects of keeping the commandments do not suf-*
> *fice to heal the powers of the soul completely. They must*
> *be complemented by a contemplative activity appro-*
> *priate to these faculties and this activity must penetrate*
> *the spirit.*[6]

### MEDITATION

The Bible is extremely important to most Protestants, so as a Lutheran child, I got a good-sized dose of it. Not only did we memorize whole psalms and entire chapters of the New Testament, but we also memorized the Apostle's Creed, the Nicene Creed, and the Lord's Prayer, along with all their meanings as recorded in the Lutheran Catechism. In Sunday school, we started with the parables of Jesus, and by the time we were young teens, we were engaged in in-depth Bible study. We were also strongly encouraged to read the Bible "straight through" in order to get a good feel for the whole story leading up to the crucifixion.

I was raised to think of the Bible as food for the intellect, a treasure house of moral values, and a precious artifact to be defended during arguments with nonbelievers. Strangely, I was never taught that the Bible can also speak to us on an intimate, personal level or lead to union with God. I first heard about this alternate way to approach scripture from the monks, who called it lectio divina or divine reading. They explained that lectio is an ancient Christian practice that actually constitutes a form of meditative prayer.

I was so used to thinking of biblical passages as something to be deciphered intellectually that it was nearly impossible to comprehend what the monks were talking about. But once I understood that lectio is a key monastic practice, I set out to learn as much as I could.

The Benedictine Fr. Luke Dysinger explains that the art of lectio divina

> begins with cultivating the ability to listen deeply, to hear "with the ear of our hearts" as St. Benedict encourages us in the Prologue to the Rule. When we read the Scriptures we should try to imitate the prophet Elijah. We should allow ourselves to become women and men who are able to listen for the still, small voice of God (1 Kings 19:12); the "faint murmuring sound" which is God's word for us, God's voice touching our hearts.[7]

Thus, the first step in lectio is to quietly, slowly, and patiently read and reread a short passage from the Bible until a particular phrase or word comes into special focus. Writer Christine Valters Painter uses the term "shimmering" to describe the way this word begins to connect with our consciousness.

The second step is *meditatio*, in which we begin to ruminate on the reading, imitating as we do the young mother of Jesus, who, upon hearing the message of the angels via the shepherds, "kept all these things, reflecting on them in her heart" (Lk 2:19). To ruminate is to ponder humbly, without the illusion that we can or even should be able to quickly grasp the deep spiritual meaning of the words. Instead, we let them sink into our hearts and become part of us, watching as they begin to interact with our memories, our hurts, and our hopes.

The third step in lectio divina is *oratio*, or prayer. We respond to God about what we have just encountered in his special word to us, and we surrender whatever part of ourselves this word has touched. This could be an old wound, never quite healed, or a doubt we have harbored for years. It could be a longing, still unmet, or a hope cruelly dashed. It could also be a secret spiritual aspiration, one we've been too embarrassed to admit before. Whatever it is, it will be deeply personal and the result of a surprising insight coming directly from rumination on his Word. It often involves a call of some kind.

Finally, we reach the stage called *contemplatio*, where we simply hold the words in our heart and rest in God's presence. At this stage, we let go of all the images that have arisen in us during the earlier stages of lectio divina. We stop thinking about ourselves and what we believe God is asking us to do. Instead, we sink into the mystery of a wordless darkness, free of images, symbols, and thoughts. We listen to the silence.

For ancient Christians, lectio was a tried-and-true method of prayer that could lead to union with God. Rumination on the Word of God prepared the heart to receive him. As I look back on my early childhood training, I am grateful to have been taught one aspect of lectio divina without knowing it. Memorization of scripture itself requires hours of patient repetition. Certain words and phrases stand out and become touchstones, helping us to remember them years later. Monastic tradition would say these touchstones are very likely words or phrases we need to ruminate on, to pray about, and to sit with in the presence of God.

### PRACTICE

Today, spend a little time reading more about the practice of lectio divina. When you feel as though it makes sense to you, look up the key passages for the day in the daily missal, or online. Choose one of these to use for lectio, and then take it to your place of prayer. Because it is a form of meditation, it's important that you give it plenty of quiet, uninterrupted time.

Sit here while I go over there and pray. (Mt 26:36)

## Saturday: Learn How to Do an Examen of Conscience

*A certain brother asked Abba Sisoes: "Counsel me, Father, for I have fallen to sin. What am I to do?"*

*The Elder said to him: "When you fall, get up again."*

*With bitterness the sinning brother continued: "Ah! Father I got up, yet I fell to the same sin again."*

*The Elder, so as not to discourage the brother, answered: "Then get up again and again."*[8]

### MEDITATION

A married friend, a former Jesuit novice, recently confided that one of the best disciplines he'd learned from his seven years in seminary was how to do a nightly examen of conscience. "But I've lost it now," he told me sadly. "Once we started having kids and I really got going in my career, I was just too tired in the evenings to think about anything but sleep. The examen is great, but after a hard day at the office, it feels too much like work."

Like all spiritual disciplines, the examen is work—there's no way around it—but it's work directed at a worthy goal: genuine self-knowledge. When thought of in this way, the ancient examen, urged upon new believers by St. Paul in 1 Corinthians and picked up later by saints Basil, Augustine, and Bernard in their respective Rules, begins to sound strangely contemporary. For what is more important to we modern types than the question, Who am I? And how many hours do we already devote to self-analysis or therapy sessions?

Such practices usually do pay off in terms of greater self-awareness. But ultimately, the examen looks beyond our individual psychological quirks to our identity as creatures made in the divine image and likeness. It illuminates those places over which we've planted a "no trespassing" sign. It sheds light on the many ways we are still very much unlike the Christ we claim to follow.

Thus, even though the examen is highly personal, it is not individualistic; it focuses not so much on our uniqueness as on our shared identity as children of God. Jesus explains what this means:

> You are my friends if you do what I command you. I no longer call you slaves, because a slave does not know what his master is doing. I have called you friends, because I have told you everything I have heard from my Father. It was not you who chose me, but I who chose you and appointed you to go and bear fruit that will remain, so that whatever you ask the Father in my name he may give you. (Jn 15:14–16)

St. Ignatius of Loyola, founder of the Jesuits, included the examen of conscience in his Spiritual Exercises, which were designed to help anybody, lay and religious alike, live a more holy life. The first step is to remember that we are in the presence of God, a spiritual fact that is surprisingly easy to forget. The second is to give thanks for all the blessings in our lives, and particularly for specific answers to prayer. The third is to recognize the work that the Holy Spirit has already done and is currently doing in our lives. As we make this inward look, we should avoid both self-condemnation or smug pats on the back.

Once we've come to a realistic view of what's going on inside, it's time to examine how we are living this particular day. Are we acting freely—that is, are we following Christ's lead—or are we being swept along by our own emotions and inner turmoil? Are we acting out of love or out of self-centered egoism? Most of the time, we discover a combination of both.

When things have come clear, we pray for reconciliation with God and whomever we may have wronged, and we resolve to stop sinning in these specific ways.

As Jesus' friends, we are involved in an ongoing effort to become more and more like our spiritual mentor and moral exemplar. Conversely, when we temporarily forget who we are, we revert to acting solely on our own. The examen of conscience can become a daily reminder of our true identity.

## PRACTICE

Today, choose a particular time, whether noon or early evening, to make an examen. You can follow the short version I've laid out in the preceding meditation, find a copy of St. Ignatius's Spiritual Exercises, or go to the Internet, where a number of websites describe the process in greater detail. Remember, you are not making this examen in preparation for Confession but instead as a form of devotion and, possibly, as a new daily practice. You may thus find it helpful to focus on one particular weakness—say, impatience—and then evaluate your day in terms of when and under what circumstances you succumbed. When you pray for reconciliation, don't forget to also make a resolve to stop caving in to this particular temptation.

> In the world you will have trouble, but take courage, I have conquered the world. (Jn 16:33)

# fourth week of lent:
## SIMPLIFYING THE SCHEDULE

The desert dwellers believed that structure rooted them and helped them grow strong. Jesus preached that it is what we do that eventually determines who we are.

## Monday: Skip a Purely Social Gathering Today

*Another Elder gave the following advice: "When you perceive that visitors are coming to visit you, before they knock on your door pray these words to God: 'O Lord, protect all of us from judgment and from evil tongues, that my brothers might depart this place in peace and gratified.'"*[1]

### MEDITATION

For many years, I was a very busy woman. Not only did I work day and night to fulfill my ambition of becoming a famous writer, but I also had academic goals: I wanted to be a tenured professor without having to first earn a PhD. With four small children to support, it was economically impossible for me to go back to grad school, so my only hope was to work my way up through the system by publishing so much my department would be forced to dispense with the usual degree requirements. Meanwhile, I focused on making myself indispensable.

What did this mean? I volunteered for committees and special commissions; I paid my own way to academic seminars; I got involved with launching a new degree program; I taught classes nobody else wanted. Most of all, I socialized. Some weeks, I was gone nearly every evening: a writer's group here, a reading there, a book launch party for a colleague, a performance put on by someone else's students, an on-campus concert, or a political focus group. I didn't particularly enjoy being out every night—by the end of most teaching days, I was exhausted. Mike, still teaching full time himself, flatly refused to accompany me to most events— but tenaciously I clung to the notion that it was Important to Be Seen. If I were to skip these gatherings, I thought, I'd soon become invisible—and then how would I ever accomplish my goals?

St. Benedict was well aware of the destruction fierce ambition can wreak in our souls. Thus, steps Six, Seven, and Eight on his ladder of humility have to do with letting go of our social and professional ambitions and learning to be

**Hold ID... BIE    2007**
**Hold Until: 02/15/17**

**NOR Hold Slip**
**Simplifying the so**

content with anonymity. Trappist Francis Kline, abbot of Mepkin Abbey, explains how this worked in his own life:

> Where I once boasted, though modestly of course, about my former skill in classical languages, in [*sic*] my exploits in carpentry, my dates with the rich and famous, as one who has had a career will do, I now appreciate and adopt a reserve. Since I am not playing the game the others are, they ignore me, think me gone dry, or out of step. . . . Instead, I must be content with the polite dismissal of the me who used to be, when my fur was shiny, when I was the center of attention.[2]

In my case, the extensive socializing was almost solely ambition fueled. Left to my own devices, I'd have much preferred time alone to think and write. Sure enough, once I began to actively resist the allure of ambitious dreams, the urge to socialize diminished very quickly. Certainly not everyone goes to social events for the reasons I did. I also do not mean to imply that all "light" social interaction is by its very nature spiritually suspect. We are drawn to casual gatherings for a variety of reasons: to distract ourselves from the pain of loneliness; to recharge our batteries when we are exhausted or depressed; or to continually connect with new and interesting people. Regardless of why we socialize, however, the fact remains that overdoing it on the social scene is like relying on tasty but sugar- and fat-saturated food: such goodies offer momentary, and sometimes even intense, pleasure, but in the long run, little real nutrition.

The monastic alternative—the observance of feast days at regular intervals throughout an otherwise quiet, abstemious life—can replace conventional socializing with celebrations of community love. As I became more involved with the monks of New Camaldoli, I found myself longing to be with them during the major feast days of the church year. Unlike most of the gallivanting I'd done in the past, which was almost entirely me-centered (Am I attractive enough? Bright enough? Witty enough? Are people noticing what a gift I am to the department?), monastic feast days point beyond the fussy preoccupations of the self to that which is universal and enduring.

## PRACTICE

Today, sit out a social event you had planned to attend. If there is nothing on your calendar, then cancel an RSVP you have already made. Notice how you feel when you deliberately withdraw from the crowd. Do you feel guilty for not fulfilling your social obligation? Do you feel sad or deprived for having missed it? Does it make you feel nervous that friends or relatives got together and you were not there?

Meditate on what socializing means to you and how difficult it would be to give it up entirely or even to cut back. What is the main benefit you reap from it? What might have to change in you for you to be able to forego most social events?

The kingdom of God is at hand. (Mk 1:15)

## Tuesday: Welcome an Interruption Today

*Once two brethren came to a certain elder whose custom it was not to eat every day. But when he saw the brethren he invited them with joy to dine with him, saying: Fasting has its reward, but he who eats out of charity fulfills two commandments, for he sets aside his own will and he refreshes his hungry brethren.*[3]

### MEDITATION

Years before my return to faith, I got caught up in the dream of becoming a famous writer of literary masterpieces. Mike and I, who had both been through divorces, were newly married then, and our children were still very young. The challenges we faced—custody issues, child support, legal debt, and lots of unresolved emotions from the past—seemed overwhelming, so I chose to escape by dwelling on my beautiful dream.

I also escaped physically by withdrawing every time I got a chance to my little office off the bedroom, which Mike had fashioned out of a former closet by installing a big window and a desk. There, at my computer, I could completely separate from the harsh realities of life. My excuse was that I "needed to write," and heaven help anyone who dared interrupt that sacrosanct time.

Two people who regularly did were my new in-laws, Mike's parents. They lived nearby, they wanted to stay in touch with their oldest son, and they missed my little stepdaughters, their grandchildren. Often on a Sunday afternoon when the girls were in town, they'd simply drop by unannounced. Since I taught full time during the week, Sunday afternoons were when I did most of my writing, and, frustrated at how little time I had to develop my "creative genius," I grew fiercely protective of these hours. Thus, when I heard my in-laws at the door, I completely lost it. My anger invariably spilled over onto poor Mike when he finally came to let me know we had company. "They're here again?" I would hiss. "Why can't they call ahead like normal people? Besides, they're not here to see me—it's you and the girls they care about. Tell them I'm gone!"

But, of course, they knew I was there. By the time I got to the living room, I'd usually composed my face and voice, but my hugs were invariably stiff and phony, which of course made them ill at ease and unsure of themselves. In their confusion, they confined their conversation with me to safe superficialities. I was furious. How could they waste my time this way? How could they not see what they were so casually interrupting each week? Why should I have to put up with their oblivious behavior time after frustrating time? It never even crossed my mind that their efforts to be friends with me were sincere.

Eventually, with the advent of God back in my life, I began to feel quite differently about my writing. No longer did it dominate my every waking moment; no longer did I yearn, as I once had, to write the Great American Novel. As my attitude about creative work began to change, so did my posture toward what I had once thought of as "interruptions." I began to feel compunction for rejecting the many overtures of my in-laws and looked for ways to heal the wounded relationship. By the time they were old and frail enough to be in need of serious help, I was grateful for the chance to be there for them.

Sadly, however, I could see that this old attitude of mine had caused some serious damage. At the very time my mother-in-law, who had five sons and no daughters, needed desperately to lean on me, the shadows of the past got subtly in the way. She was always kind and gentle, but I knew that she could not quite trust my love for her—not after so many years of those stiff and phony hugs at the front door.

The Catholic philosopher Josef Pieper defines love as the ability to turn to another individual and say, "It's good that you exist!"[4] People are sensitive; they know when their welcome is genuine and when it is not. They sense the warmth, and they know when it is lacking. True hospitality—opening one's arms to an interruption—cannot be faked.

I spent two hours alone with my mother-in-law the day she died. She was light as air by then, and consciousness had long since flown, but something in her still clung to life. As I watched her struggles to breathe, I felt guilt for the times I'd rejected her well-meant advances. I prayed that she'd been able to forgive me for those hard years between us and that she'd come to believe I loved her after all.

### PRACTICE

Today, prepare yourself for an interruption, and if it comes, see if you can welcome it for the sake of love. If nobody comes to the door, then meditate instead on your attitude toward unexpected visitors. Look in particular at the way you offer hospitality, especially when it is inconvenient. Think about what takes priority in your heart. Then ask to be given the gift of welcoming whomever God sends your way.

Love your neighbor as yourself. (Mt 19:19)

## Wednesday: Today, Pray the Divine Office

*Abba Matoes said, "I prefer a light and steady activity, to one that is painful at the beginning but is soon broken off."*[5]

### MEDITATION

I was an oblate for many years before I tried to pray the way the monks do: in a series of structured prayer times traditionally known as the "Divine Office," or Liturgy of the Hours, beginning before daylight and ending at nightfall. On retreat at the hermitage, it was no problem; everything in the environment was conducive to organized prayer. At home, it was a different story, so I quietly forgot about chanting the psalms on a regular basis unless I happened to be with the monks. Even then, I generally wound up skipping dawn Vigils, which begins at 5:30 a.m., in favor of some extra sleep.

Yet, after two or three days in a row of morning Lauds, midday Eucharist, and evening Vespers at the hermitage, I always felt different. For a while, I attributed this sense of renewal to being in the company of the monks, or to the beauty of the Big Sur wilderness. It finally occurred to me, however, that there could be another reason for feeling transformed: I'd come into close contact with the shaping force of monastic life—what St. Benedict calls the "Work of God," or scheduled, communal times of prayer.

Benedict devotes a large part of the Rule to developing a framework for daily worship. Everything else, including running a guesthouse, hearing confessions, and leading the community, must give way to this essential monastic vocation. St. Romuald adds in the Camaldolese Brief Rule, "The path you must follow is in the Psalms—never leave it. If you have just come to the monastery, and in spite of your good will you cannot accomplish what you want, then take every opportunity you can to sing the Psalms in your heart and to understand them with your mind."[6]

Filled with new zeal, I bought the Camaldolese psalter, translated from the Italian, which covers Lauds and Vespers. I copied out the Psalm schedule for Vigils by hand. I made a plan to go to daily Mass at a nearby church. And I pledged to myself that I would follow the schedule of the monks if it killed me.

The sheer doggedness of my determination should have been a red flag. Despite my spiritual director's cautionary words about my already overflowing schedule, I counted on teeth-gritting discipline to get me through. And for a week, this worked. Every day I'd get up early, settle myself in the big green chair with my morning cup of decaf, and dig in. Evenings were a little trickier; I was always tired by then, and it was hard not to get sleepy and lose track. But I persevered.

By the end of week two, however, I was starting to falter. I'd pretty much dropped Vespers by then and was starting to think about combining Vigils and Lauds. So what if I didn't do them till midmorning or even noon sometimes? The point was that I was doing them. Or was that the point? What, actually, was the point?

These last two questions were what derailed my heroic attempt to live like a monk despite my already full householder schedule. This refusal to face the facts about my life as it was made me a sitting duck for what used to be known as the "noonday demon," or *acedia*: the thought that mocks spiritual effort as futile. A few weeks later, I dropped the project entirely, avoiding the psalter and telling myself I could do my devotions in a different, more reasonable way. What that might be, I didn't know.

The result was drift: I didn't have an established practice of my own, and I knew I could not maintain the one kept by the monks. Discouraged, I went back to the hermitage to see if I could find some direction. There, I noticed as if for the first time something I must have observed on countless occasions before: not everybody came to every service. Even monks did not pray the Hours religiously.

Obviously, it was okay to make some realistic adjustments to my own schedule of devotions. This was not meant to be an "all or nothing" project. However, even the most minimal, daily practice required a basic change I'd been unwilling to make before: I needed to take a hard look at the length of my to-do list. If I were to incorporate at least one of the Hours into my daily round, then life had to give way in some measure to the Psalms.

Wiggling free of important obligations was not easy. Whenever I thought about passing on a responsibility to someone else, or saying no to a request, I felt guilty. But with some trepidation, I made changes that allowed me to establish a new pattern. The result? An infinitesimally slow formation process that illumines my life with a quiet beauty I could not imagine until I pledged faithfulness to the practice.

### PRACTICE

Today, go to your private prayer place and recite one of the daily Hours on your own. You can find versions of these in a daily missal or online; you could also buy or borrow a breviary that contains the full service. You can speak the words out loud or repeat them silently, though if you do, it helps to move your lips. If you have ever heard the Psalms chanted and have a breviary with musical notations, you could also try singing them to yourself.

> Why are you sleeping? Get up and pray that you
> may not undergo the test. (Lk 22:46)

## Thursday: Go to Morning Mass Today

*One can see them scattered in the desert waiting for Christ like loyal sons watching for their father, or like an army expecting its emperor, or like a sober household looking forward to the arrival of its master and liberator.*[7]

### MEDITATION

"Are you a believer?" My questioner was a seller of cashews at a corner stand in Old Jerusalem. Surprised, I nodded, but this was apparently not good enough. "Do you believe much?" he persisted.

"I do. I am a serious believer." Satisfied, he took my shekels and handed me my bag of nuts. Later I wondered: what does this question mean in a place like Israel, where only two percent of the population is Christian? Did he think I was Jewish or Muslim? Did it even matter to him? After a few days in this remarkable place, I concluded that, political problems aside, it probably did not. For Jerusalem has to be one of the most spiritually charged places on earth, and what he really wanted to know was this: are you here to worship the God we all share? Or are you simply here to gawk?

Each morning I woke to the muezzins' ululating call to prayer. On Friday afternoons, devout Muslims in their finest clothes streamed out of the Damascus Gate after worship. At the Western Wall, Orthodox Jews placed folded slips of paper between the ancient blocks of stone, their foreheads touching the wall in reverence. Armenian monks in pointed black hoods moved their lips in prayer as they strode down narrow lanes, and shrouded Ethiopians made their devotions on the roof of the Holy Sepulchre. In the Old City, religion saturates each waking moment.

Not so in America, where much of the landscape has been stripped of meaningful religious symbolism and filled instead with emporia devoted to consumption. Not so in our hypercompetitive society where to be human too often means to be a producer of goods and services rather than a unique person, made in the image of God. In this spiritually parched environment, we can easily get caught up in a scramble for survival and a desperate search for meaning, forgetting that our lives are already rich and significant beyond measure, thanks to the dynamic relationship we enjoy with a Creator who loves us.

Back home from Jerusalem, I felt lost and sad. As much as I adored my family and friends and as much as I enjoyed my career, something that sustained life had gone missing. Where were the vibrant religious practices I had witnessed every day on the streets of the ancient city? Where were the public prayers, the silent prostrations, the murmured blessings as people passed one another in the narrow alleyways? The modern secular world seemed bleak beyond belief, and I longed for a return to the land of spirit.

Glumly, I went to Mass, which had always had the power to cheer me in the past. And suddenly, as though I'd never gotten it before, I "saw" in a new way what had been going on there from earliest Christian times: the myriad symbols, pregnant with meaning, the strangely anonymous yet totally communal joy, the ancient, vibrating connection with another realm. For the first time, I understood that Mass is not merely a beautiful ritual but is instead a genuine mystical experience, an intense moment of full communion with God.

"Almighty God, we pray that your angel may take this sacrifice to your altar in heaven," says the priest, and instantly we are connected to all those who have believed and died before us and all those who abide in realms we cannot yet fathom. We have passed through the shimmering membrane that divides the created world from the universe of spirit, and momentarily, we are transported. And then, as we partake of the Body and the Precious Blood, we see with startling clarity that we truly do remain in Christ and he in us and that, through us, he is still working his miracles here on earth.

But how often, in this world of distraction, do we forget? Hence, the monastic practice of daily Eucharist and its constant renewal of the mystical connection to God. The Mass replenishes our soul and nourishes our being in a mysterious but absolutely discernible way. Daily Mass answers the cashew seller's question—Do you believe?—with a yes that is grounded in lived experience rather than in intellectual assent alone.

### PRACTICE

If you are not already in the habit of going to weekday Mass, then try it out today. Most parishes offer at least one opportunity Monday through Saturday, often in the morning before people must go to work. Sometimes an evening Vespers service may co-opt that day's Mass, so it's good to check ahead of time. Notice how much quieter and more reverent a weekday Mass can be; with fewer people and a simpler service, the atmosphere undergoes a subtle shift from that of Sunday. Before Eucharist begins, pray for the ability to really "see" what is going on during this ancient sacramental rite.

> I am the living bread that came down from heaven; whoever eats this bread will live forever; and the bread that I will give is my flesh for the life of the world. (Jn 6:51)

## Friday: Take a Walk and Say the Rosary Today

*Just as bread is nourishment for the body and virtue for the soul, so is spiritual prayer nourishment for the intelligence.*[8]

### MEDITATION

When I became a Catholic twenty-plus years ago, one of the first things I learned was how to say the Rosary. My teachers were four women friends who had been taught the prayer when they were children and had never abandoned the practice. At the time we formed our Rosary group, we were all working mothers with young teenagers. We'd meet at 5:30 p.m. in the Old Mission garden, just as the sun was beginning to set, and we'd sit on a low stone wall and a long wooden bench that faced each other.

We didn't have a lot of time—there were kids to pick up from soccer practice and, after that, dinner to make—but what we had, we used for the prayer. One of the women, Anna, always said it in Spanish; the rest of the group used contemporary English. I myself was drawn to the cadences of an older version: "Hail Mary, full of grace, blessed art thou among women and blessed is the fruit of thy womb, Jesus."

The setting beneath a dramatic peak, black against the twilit sky, was beautiful, the roses that surrounded us were fragrant, and I loved my four friends. Though at first the prayer felt foreign to me, the fact that it was as familiar as breathing to the rest of the group gradually put me at my ease. It seemed appropriate that five mothers should be devoting some time to the mother of Jesus.

Learning that the words of the prayer were not written by medieval Marian devotees, as I'd always thought, but instead came straight from the Bible, also helped me feel more comfortable. At the Annunciation, the angel Gabriel greets Mary with the words, "Hail, favored one! The Lord is with you" (Lk 1:28). And when the newly pregnant Mary goes to visit her cousin Elizabeth, herself heavy with child, the babe inside Elizabeth leaps, and Elizabeth, "filled with the holy Spirit," cries out, "Most blessed are you among women, and blessed is the fruit of your womb" (Lk 1:41–42). Until I began to say the prayer, I'd never thought much about the key women in Jesus' life and the fact that they were individually called into difficult service by God in the same way that the great patriarchs and prophets of the Old Testament were called.

Once our weekly Rosary meetings had become a regular fixture in my life, I found myself wanting to say the prayer more often. By then, a friend had given me a beautiful gift: a silver and turquoise set of Rosary beads I carried in the car. Soon I found myself with a new habit: praying the Rosary as I drove. Then one morning out on my daily walk, I found myself whispering, "Hail Mary, full of grace, the Lord is with thee . . ." and realized the prayer had now taken up its abode in another area of my life. Like the "Jesus Prayer" of the Orthodox Church, the Rosary seemingly has the ability to root itself so firmly in our hearts that it becomes second nature to us.

When our oldest daughter was about to go into labor with her first child, she asked if I'd be present, along with her husband, in the delivery room. The labor was extremely long and difficult and finally ended in a late-night C-section. But the baby was fine, and after a few days, we were told we could make the hour-long drive from the hospital in the mountains back to their home in the valley.

Strapping a newborn into a car seat for his first ride is always a little nervous-making, and the situation was made doubly stressful by the fact that none of the adults had gotten much sleep during the past week. By the time we got mother and baby situated, the sun was beginning to go down and the twisting mountain road was getting darker. Sitting in the back beside my newest grandchild, I automatically crossed myself and began to whisper the Rosary.

My son-in-law, whose ears must have been sharpened by anxiety, swiveled in the driver's seat. "Did you just say something?"

"Well," I said, "it's just that the monks have this habit, and I've picked it up, of saying the Rosary whenever they leave on a dangerous journey. But don't worry—I'll just whisper it to myself, okay?"

"No!" he commanded. "Say it loud enough that I can hear it!" So I did, twice, until we had made it safely down the mountain.

Twenty years later, the original Rosary group has long since disbanded. Somebody moved away, someone else got sick, and in the way of busy modern people, we gradually stopped meeting. But the prayer lives on: I say it every day, and I suspect my friends do, too. As soon as they are old enough, I'll teach it to my grandchildren, including Eli, who descended the mountain at three days old.

### PRACTICE

If you are not already familiar with the Rosary, look it up today on the Internet. Read it through once before you actually pray it, noticing the beautiful scriptural language. Think about Mary, the unmarried young girl who said yes to God and thus opened herself to public shaming and possible rejection. Ask yourself if you have ever been asked by God to do something difficult. What was your answer? Did you carry out the requested task?

Once you have familiarized yourself with the prayer, print it out and take it to your special place. Then, quiet your mind and heart and go slowly through each decade. The Rosary is an oral prayer, meant to be spoken out loud, but it lends itself especially well to a quiet murmur.

Behold, your mother. (Jn 19:27)

## Saturday: Invite a Lonely Person in for Tea and Conversation

*When Father Apollo heard the sound of singing, he greeted us according to the custom which all the brethren follow. When he saw us, he first prostrated, lying full length on the ground; then getting up he kissed us, and having brought us in, prayed for us; then, after washing our feet with his own hands, he invited us to partake of some refreshment. He does this with all the brethren who come to visit him.*[9]

### MEDITATION

Fr. Michael's voice on the phone was apologetic. "Got an assignment for the God Squad," he said. "I need you to house someone for at least three days, and he doesn't have a car, can't pay you for gas, but will need to be driven back and forth to a job site."

I gulped. "Okaaay."

"He's been out of work the past few years, and now he's been offered a chance to prove himself. He's also been through a rather strange experience. He'll get over it, but right now he's a bit . . . wound up. Can I count on you?"

By now this was sounding like the opening to a thriller, which is part of the reason Fr. Michael is irresistible, so I signed off with the agreement that I'd pick up our new houseguest the following day.

Vassily turned out to be a recent immigrant who'd been offered a job in America and moved his family to the States. Before he could find and pay for a health insurance policy, he'd been in a devastating accident that put him in the hospital for months. The bills were monumental. He could no longer work. Worse, one of his injured legs deteriorated to the point that the doctors wanted to amputate. Through the power of prayer (he'd give us no details, having been sworn to secrecy), he'd been completely healed.

At this point in his story, he leaped from the table and pulled up his pants leg to reveal a spindly stick of a limb, crisscrossed with flamingo-pink scars. "This very leg," he almost shouted. "You can see for yourself how bad it was." And began hopping around the room to show us just how thorough the healing had been.

Of course, we were fascinated but also concerned. He was clearly emotionally unstable, and we were not sure how best to help him. But we took him to the guest room and told him we were at his service.

"I must be on the job site at 7:00 a.m. tomorrow morning!" he said. "I will need you to drive me!"

We did. But at the end of the three days we were so burned out with his high-octane angst, which seemed sure to ruin any chance he had at getting hired, that we rented him a motel room and gave him the cash to get back home on his own. We were not proud of ourselves. It appeared that our hospitality was a meager thing, incapable of coping with the unemployed recipients of miraculous healings. Grumbling and exhausted and blaming one another for this frustrating debacle, we tried our best to forget poor Vassily and move on. Yet, I couldn't help wondering if we'd missed the point entirely.

When Mother Teresa was asked why she bothered to take in people on the verge of death, she responded, "Once upon a time, a good man returned a fish to the water. People told him: 'So what? You save one fish. Tomorrow the sea will drop hundreds onto the shore. What difference did you make?' The man answered: 'For that single fish, I made all the difference in the world. I saved him.'"[10]

The Rule of St. Benedict enshrines hospitality as a primary Christian duty because the world is full of stranded fish, men like our trying houseguest, people who ache for the smallest sign that someone cares enough to be inconvenienced for their sakes. It might have helped if we'd realized that what Vassily really needed from us had more to do with compassion than solutions to his many problems. We might have experienced less guilty frustration at our inability to "help" him and more inclination to simply be there for him, however briefly, as he struggled on with his difficult life.

### PRACTICE

Today, think about someone who lives alone and could use a warm cup of tea and some friendly conversation. Perhaps it is an elderly neighbor down the street. Or maybe it is simply a person who is hard to get along with, someone without many social skills. Offer hospitality in whatever way seems appropriate, noticing any resistance you might have to opening your life up this way, no matter how temporarily. Are you worried about being asked for wisdom you don't have? Are you afraid you will be expected to make an ongoing commitment to this person? Or is it simply a matter of the disruption such a gesture might cause in your schedule?

> [Jesus said], "Which of these three, in your opinion, was neighbor to the robbers' victim?"
>
> He answered, "The one who treated him with mercy."
> Jesus said to him, "Go and do likewise." (Lk 10:36–37)

# fifth week of lent:
## SIMPLIFYING RELATIONSHIPS

The desert dwellers practiced "golden silence" in order to listen better for God's still, small voice—and to limit the damage they did with their tongues. Jesus taught that we are to love one another as he first loved us.

## Monday: Spend an Hour in Solitude Today

*Abba Isaiah questioned Abba Macarius saying, "Give me a word." The old man said to him, "Flee from men." Abba Isaiah said to him, "What does it mean to flee from men?" The old man said, "It means to sit in your cell and weep for your sins."* [1]

### MEDITATION

Mike loves sailing. For years he dreamed of sailing alone around the world. When the opportunity failed to present itself, he resorted to reading about other people's quests instead. I used to ask him what it was about single-handed sailing that drew him so deeply, but he couldn't put it into words. For a long time, I assumed that his dream of solitude upon the high seas was about taking on an exciting challenge and winning. I couldn't imagine why else you'd deliberately court months of frigid, frightening loneliness in the middle of nowhere—not, at least, until I'd been through a version of it myself.

One day, sometime after all our kids had left home, Mike was invited to help crew a trimaran in the Sea of Cortez, off the coast of Baja California. He did not know the owner well, but he eagerly accepted. First they would have to trailer the boat nearly four hundred miles south. Then they would be completely out of touch for the following five days as they sailed among desert islands. I didn't want him to go—all I could think of were the various disasters that might befall him on this journey, not to mention how lonely I'd be in his absence—but I knew how long he'd been waiting for a chance like this. Though he wouldn't be circumnavigating the globe as he'd always dreamed, I could see that, as far as he was concerned, a week-long sail in isolated waters was a great consolation prize. Putting on a brave front, I kissed him goodbye and told him to have a great trip.

The moment he was gone and the house went silent, I was filled with the conviction that he would never return from this adventure, that the boat would sink in the middle of nowhere, and I'd never see or hear from him again. Misery seeped into my bones, and I found myself almost unable to function. And this sense of profound bereavement would not lift, no matter how much I told myself to snap out of it. Worse, I was so embarrassed about what was happening to me, I couldn't bring myself to call anyone for help.

The desert dwellers were deliberately courting this state of lonely grief when they left behind their families, friends, and positions in the world to head into the wilderness. Solitude precipitated a radical stripping of everything they'd learn to count on in their former lives. For some of them, at least, this meant learning to endure a grinding, seemingly purposeless isolation, the likes of which most of us cannot imagine.

Yet, as James Cowan points out, the painful severance of relationships undergone by desert solitaries like St. Anthony the Great also opened the door to a new way of being:

> This lonely man living in the desert imposed a new valuation on human endeavor: that people had a right to an inner life over and above their responsibilities as social beings. Such a premise went far beyond any that Socrates had proposed, even at his death. A new force had entered the world. By his retreat into the desert, Anthony paved the way for others to take their first step on the road to selflessness.[2]

The price for this kind of liberation, however, is incredibly steep. Solitude brings us face to face with a person who fills us with dismay: our naked and unadorned self. Instead of the self-sufficient, goal-directed, accomplished human being we've learned to secretly admire, we are suddenly revealed as a weak, dependent, fearful creature who much of the time uses others to fulfill desperate needs. If we have prided ourselves on the maturity of our faith, solitude twitches back the curtain on self-deception. The experience can be devastating.

In my case, Mike's sailing adventure triggered a solitude-related spiritual crisis for which I was completely unprepared. For three days, I reeled in the face of overwhelming sorrow and despair. I tried to pray but could not focus. I tried to read but could not comprehend. It was only when I got stomach flu and couldn't eat or drink either that I finally got it: God was teaching me a crucial spiritual lesson.

Until I faced up to the inadequacy of my self-constructed social identity and understood that much of what I called "love" was actually fearful dependence on others, especially Mike, I could not truly comprehend the good news of the gospels. I was indeed made for community, though not the one to which I so fiercely clung. No matter how beautiful and precious, my earthly relationships, doomed from the beginning to be interrupted by death, were meant to point me toward my true family—the Body of Christ.

Too sick with the flu and imagined bereavement to take care of myself, I finally called a friend, a fellow oblate who told me in no uncertain terms, "You need to eat. What do you have in the house?"

Fuzzy-headed, I thought for a minute. "Carrots?"

"Then eat a carrot," she said. "Now."

Gratefully—it was so good to let go of my own confused thinking at this point and simply obey—I followed her orders. A few days later when Mike got home, I was no longer sick, and the temptation was to simply forget about the awful experience I'd been through in his absence. Yet, I knew I could not; hidden in that solitary suffering was a pearl I needed to find and cherish.

### PRACTICE

Today, spend an hour in solitude: no phone, no e-mail, no TV, and no interaction with another human being, live or electronic. Prayerfully imagine yourself on an extended, solitary adventure. If you are already accustomed to living by yourself, think about the ways in which you defend yourself against loneliness. Do you rely on the TV to keep you company? Do you spend a lot of time calling friends? Do you feel compelled to socialize often? Ask God to show you what you'd prefer not to see: your undefended self. Then ask God to strengthen and sustain you.

> Amen, I say to you, there is no one who has given
> up house or wife or brothers or parents or chil-
> dren for the sake of the kingdom of God who will
> not receive [back] an overabundant return in this
> present age and eternal life in the age to come.
> (Lk 18:29)

## Tuesday: Sit in Silence with a Friend Today

*[An Elder] said, "Do not be humble only in speech,
but also be humble of mind; for without humility it is
impossible to be exalted in Godly works."*[3]

### MEDITATION

My first friend at the hermitage was Fr. Bernard, at the
time a vigorous, white-haired, sixty-five-year-old, one of the
original members of the community at Big Sur. A natural-
born people lover, he was assigned to the bookstore, where
guests often went in search of advice. I fell into conversation
with him on my very first retreat, and he quickly took me
under his wing.

For the next fifteen years, every time I went to the hermitage, we spent the two hours following Vespers walking down
the mountain and back. First we recited the Rosary; then we
talked. He reported what he'd heard on his shortwave radio;

I told him about the kids. He filled me in on the doings of his legendary mother, and I countered with stories about Mike. At the midpoint of our hike, we sauntered out into the middle of Pacific Coast Highway and each touched a foot to the center line.

As he approached his eighties, however, Fr. Bernard suddenly developed terrible hip pain and, after many sleepless months, underwent a joint replacement. He'd never been in a hospital before, much less undergone surgery, so I assumed the lengthy recovery might be tough on him. When he failed to rally in his old, vibrant way, I thought the operation must have shocked his system. But as it turned out, there was more going on: Fr. Bernard was experiencing the onset of Parkinson's disease.

Five years later, he can still get around without a walker, but he's become frail and unsteady, nods off during the Divine Office, and requires full-time help from a brother monk. He can only feed himself with great difficulty; his hands tremble so badly he cannot write anymore. What's no doubt been hardest for him is that he can no longer speak comprehensibly. His thick French Canadian accent is already a challenge for most listeners, but now he cannot control the movements of his throat muscles, so the words, if they do come, are so soft, breathy, and rapid that few people can follow him anymore.

No longer do we stride down the mountain together and touch our feet to the center line, nor do we recite the Rosary and discuss our lives. Instead, we shuffle slowly to one of the benches overlooking the ocean. There, we sit side by side, so close our hands are touching, and gaze upon the horizon. If at some point he decides to speak, I listen hard and sometimes I can make out bits of what he's saying. For the most part, however, we visit in poignant silence, our hearts filled with memories of a long and precious friendship now entering its final stage.

"Silence can be a mini-experience of death and resurrection," says Episcopalian priest and psychologist Morton Kelsey. "It is a temporary cessation of one's doing and planning and desires. When we actually die, we give up the possessions that have mattered to us and entrust them to the care of others. Much the same thing happens when one stops in silence."[4]

For Fr. Bernard, this silent communion of ours is not only a humble acquiescence to his own approaching death but also represents a return to an earlier, more rigorous and much-loved time in his long monastic life. When he first became a monk, silence reigned supreme and speech was kept to an absolute minimum. For a naturally gregarious person like him, it must have been a grueling discipline, but in time he came to embrace it. And this long schooling in the art of silence and "golden solitude," as the Camaldolese call it, is now serving him well. Despite his inability to speak, he has no trouble whatsoever expressing his love for old friends like me.

### PRACTICE

Today, think about someone with whom you'd feel comfortable spending some time in silence. Then call and make arrangements to meet in a beautiful, peaceful place. To avoid causing unease, let this person know ahead of time what you are planning and why.

As you sit together without speaking, think about the friend beside you. What is it in particular that makes this person such a wonderful companion? What quality allows you to feel natural being together without talking? What have you learned from the friendship, and what will you miss if a time of separation comes? At the end of this exercise, tell your friend what you've been thinking about and express your gratitude for the friendship.

> A good person out of the store of goodness in his heart produces good. (Lk 6:45)

## Wednesday: Visit Someone in the Hospital

> *Abba Epiphanios used to say that the Canaanite woman wept and was heeded; the woman with an issue of blood approached in silence and was praised; the Publican did not open his mouth at all, and yet his prayer was heard by God; while the Pharisee shouted and was condemned.*[5]

## MEDITATION

For years, we've hosted a weekly Christian meditation session in our big red barn. The group changes and flows with the seasons. Some people like the long, warm, light-filled evenings of summer, even though at times it gets so hot that we have to adjourn to the turtle pond instead. Others prefer dark and rainy winter nights, when the twinkle lights strung from the eaves and a couple of electric candles provide a dim glow against the great black outdoors.

With the exception of a small and loyal core group, people have tended to come and go. One couple, however, were such regular participants that I learned to count on them if we ourselves happened to be out of town. They would arrive early, lock up the dogs, open the gate, and prepare the room for the others. Then they'd lead the meditation and close up when everyone else had left.

But one day, they failed to appear. Shortly thereafter, I got an e-mail from Martin: Evelyn, just a few years older than me, had had a massive stroke. She'd already undergone brain surgery and been placed in a medically induced coma. When, weeks later, she was finally awakened, it became clear that she was paralyzed on one side. She couldn't yet breathe on her own and thus could not speak either.

At first, I was so devastated it was hard to be with her. Every time I saw her shaved head, her motionless limbs, and the tracheotomy that kept her airway open, I superimposed the image of my laughing, vibrant fellow meditator, the friend I'd come to rely on like a sister. I felt as though she'd died but was somehow still with us in a terribly altered form. After four months, however, her condition had become the new reality, and for the first time, I really began thinking about what it must be like for her: what was happening inside as the long hours and days and weeks continued to move past. A couple of other friends and I decided to make the three-hour drive to the rehab facility where she was now staying.

"Care of the sick must rank above and before all else, so that they may truly be served as Christ," says the Rule of St. Benedict. "Let a separate room be designated for the sick, and let them be served by an attendant who is God-fearing, attentive, and concerned."[6] Benedict also asks the abbot to be a father to the sick in an even more obvious way than he is to the rest of the community. Like the poor, the very old, and the very young, the sick represent the weakest and most vulnerable among us. As such, they can be great burdens in terms of the time and energy they require. We often avoid being with them because we are loathe to "squander" our precious, limited resources on people who are sometimes too preoccupied by their own pain or disability to even notice and appreciate what we are doing.

Yet the sick are wonderful reminders that we, too, are much more fragile and dependent than we like to think. One of the reasons the very sick make us uncomfortable is because they mirror, in their ravaged flesh, hidden weaknesses in ourselves. They are too worn out by their suffering to be "productive," much less to create or generate something entirely new—or so it seems. They do not "feed" us in the way that being around vibrant youth and health can feed us. Instead, and perhaps much more importantly, they give us back the truth, which is that we, too, will come to this, if death does not take us by surprise beforehand.

Going to visit my sick friend was revelatory. Her hair was now an inch long, she was sitting up in a wheel chair, and she'd gotten back partial use of one arm and hand. More, she could now speak, though softly and haltingly, and only after much thought. We took turns pushing her chair through the rehab facility corridors, then out into a quiet Zen garden. There, we talked with her, though not in the old way, which no longer worked. We would pat her hand or arm, then ask a question. She would ponder deeply, sometimes for several minutes. Then she would breathe out a one or two-word answer.

One of these responses was astounding. When I asked her what she was praying for most, I assumed she would say "healing." Instead, after a very long pause, she offered, "Enlightenment." And suddenly I saw that she was not, in these truly agonizing circumstances, simply marking time or even sliding slowly into despair. Instead, she was waiting for what God might teach her next.

## PRACTICE

Today, visit somebody in the hospital. This person does not have to be extremely ill, or even someone you know. Simply make yourself available to anyone who might need a cheering word and a friendly face. Remind yourself beforehand that visits of this kind require patience. Don't try to skimp on time, even if being there makes you uncomfortable. Remember that you are no exception to the rule: we are all of us weak creatures, all of us subject to physical disability and death—all of us in need of love.

> Then the king will say to those on his right, "Come, you who are blessed by my Father. Inherit the kingdom prepared for you from the foundation of the world. For I was hungry and you gave me food, I was thirsty and you gave me drink, a stranger and you welcomed me, naked and you clothed me, ill and you cared for me." (Mt 25:34–36)

## Thursday: Volunteer at a Soup Kitchen Today

*[Pachomius] answered him, "The Church's rule is that we should only join together those two [days], so that we might still have the strength to accomplish without fainting the things we are commanded to do, namely,*

*unceasing prayer, vigils, reciting of God's law, and our*
*manual labor about which we have orders in the Holy*
*Scriptures and which ought to permit us to hold out*
*our hands to the poor."*[7]

### MEDITATION

Some years ago, I realized that I spent a lot of time cooking for people. With our big vegetable garden and orchard,
we usually had plenty of produce available, so it didn't cost
much, except in physical labor, to feed a crowd. Also, the
work was enjoyable; I loved spending hours in the garden, and I liked to bake and cook. Why not branch out, I
thought, and get involved with feeding a much larger group?
Why not sign up to feed the homeless?

I joined a team that had been together for many years.
Our leader was a five-foot-tall dynamo with a wicked grin
and the soul of a cheerleader. Each month, Bonnie arrived
at the homeless shelter with five gigantic pans filled with
something hot and tasty: homemade meatloaf, baked chick-
en, Italian-style lasagne, rich macaroni and cheese, and so
forth. The rest of us provided the side dishes: bread, salads,
vegetables, dessert, and beverages. For my first day on the
job, I brought two big canning pots full of taco salad made
with lettuce and tomatoes from our garden, lots of beans
and cheese, and jazzed-up Thousand Island dressing. Except
for one man who thought I'd overdone it on the dressing,

the salad was an instant hit, and from then on I was asked to bring it every time.

We usually fed about one hundred thirty people: single men and women of all ages, mothers with small children, and entire families. They began arriving at the shelter a good hour ahead of time and waited patiently in line until we were all set up inside. Then, just as the clock struck twelve and the big rolling doors were opening to display the counter filled with food, Bonnie would call out, "Let's pray!" and we'd cross ourselves and bow our heads, reciting the Lord's Prayer out loud as the first ones in line entered the building.

When people thanked us for the meal, as they often did, I noticed that Bonnie took this opportunity to give credit where it was due: "God is good," she'd say, or "God bless you!" Meanwhile, she was busy directing traffic behind the counter or ladling out hot meatballs and clearly, by the size of that wicked grin, enjoying every minute of her time on the job. The effect on the crowd was obvious: they could see that, in her eyes, it was a privilege to serve them. One full-of-fire little woman in a beaten-down, raggle-taggle group of people, many of whom saw themselves as failures and misfits, had the power to impart dignity and self-respect under circumstances that are all too often soaked in misery and shame.

St. Benedict insisted that the needy not only be fed but also treated with an extra measure of loving-kindness. "Great care and concern are to be shown in receiving poor people and pilgrims, because in them more particularly Christ is received."[8] Not only do the poor represent an opportunity to serve Christ ("For I was hungry and you gave me food"), but they also teach us how to love—that is, without thought of gratitude, reward, or reciprocal response, though often these are forthcoming. The kind of love that Jesus modeled is impossible without self-transcendence; at the very least, we must be willing to lay aside our own needs and desires to effectively serve another. Such an internal shift does not come easily or naturally, and it only comes after long practice.

Perhaps this was the secret behind the effervescent joy in our team leader: she loved the homeless because they'd taught her how to love.

### PRACTICE

Today, volunteer to serve or distribute food in a homeless shelter, food bank, or church pantry. Most parishes sponsor some kind of food distribution program and are usually happy to have help. When you arrive, notice the people waiting in line. What are their stories? Could they be you? As you serve them, thank God for the opportunity to serve Christ.

Feed my sheep. (Jn 21:17)

## Friday: Seek Out Someone Who Is Angry with You and Apologize

*"I have never lain down to sleep having some feeling of grief in my heart about my neighbor,"* Abba Agathon said. *"And, by the same token, to the extent that I could control such, I have never let another person fall asleep upset with me."*[9]

### MEDITATION

When I was still teaching at the university, I wound up on a committee with an energetic young associate professor. She shared an office with an older man, a somewhat dour lecturer who was now close to retiring. Esther was a vociferous person, filled with new-teacher zeal. I liked her, but at times her loud, exuberant laughter in the hallways made me cringe.

One day, she called and asked if I could meet with her in her office. Frank, the lecturer who shared her space, was hard at work at his desk grading papers and barely greeted me when I came in. Esther, on the other hand, was fired up, ready to tackle the latest challenge confronting our committee, and sure we would be victorious this time. Soon, she got me so wound up that we were laughing out loud.

Suddenly Frank stood up, slammed his notebook against the desk, and yelled, "How am I supposed to accomplish

anything with you two women cackling your heads off!"
Then he stomped out the door.

Stunned, Esther and I stared at each other. I felt terrible—we'd been disrespectful—but she was enraged. "How
dare he!" she said. "This is my office, too. I can say or do
whatever I want in here. He's only acting this way because
we're women."

I wasn't so sure about that. I knew Frank, and I knew he
was sensitive and easily disturbed. He'd told me once that
he felt it was grossly unfair that his status as lecturer placed
him "below" people like Esther. No doubt her loud laughter
really had made it impossible for him to concentrate on his
grading.

Very quickly, I found myself swept up in a controversy
that pulled in our department head, our dean, and finally
the union. Frank had been disrespected, and for him, it was
clearly an issue of class. Esther had been disrespected, and
for her, it was just as clearly an issue of gender. It was up
to me to testify to the truth. But the more dramatic things
became, the less I wanted to be involved. Actually, I thought
they were both being petty and egotistical and that they
needed to apologize to one another and move on.

When I finally made this suggestion, both Esther and
Frank became even angrier—this time at me. Soon, I began to feel uncomfortable walking the hallways. What if
I bumped into one of them? I found myself avoiding certain buildings, skipping committee meetings, and grading

my papers at the library downtown. Their mutual hostility might indeed be silly and egotistical, I thought, but it had poisoned the whole environment for me.

One of the most powerful passages in the gospels has to do with offending our brother. In Matthew 5:20–48 (Jesus' "hard" sayings about anger, lust, divorce, and "cutting off" those parts of us that cause us to sin), Jesus points out we can give offense in a hundred subtle and not-so-subtle ways. He draws a parallel between these acts and the great commandments against adultery and murder.

But then Jesus adds an intriguing follow-up: "Therefore, if you bring your gift to the altar, and there recall that your brother has anything against you, leave your gift there at the altar, go first and be reconciled with your brother, and then come and offer your gift" (Mt 5:23–24). This is easy enough to accept, if we have knowingly offended someone. But what if we've done nothing wrong? Do we have to be the ones who initiate reconciliation?

If one purpose of forgiving is to defuse dangerous, building anger, then this is not a difficult question: the loving thing to do, regardless of our seeming lack of culpability, is to help others return to their senses. But in fact, we often are at fault, even when we believe ourselves to be innocent. In my case, one thing I did need to apologize for was my contemptuous scoffing. Though I'd never said it out loud, their battle seemed absurd to me, and no doubt they'd picked up on this through my body language and tone of voice. Early

on, I'd stopped listening to either of them when they tried to
articulate their positions. I'd made the incorrect assumption
that they were posturing, that the issues they took so seriously—class and gender—could not possibly be that important to them. On what did I base this conclusion? On the
fact that these issues were unimportant to me, personally.

Clearly, my thinly veiled contempt had been noticed,
and it had hurt them. In the end, it did not matter whether
they were right or wrong, noble or crass; they both believed
they were fighting the good fight, and I had let them know
in a hundred subtle ways that I thought they were being
fools. I wondered how I would have reacted had they chosen
something else to fight about, something in which I had a
real stake. I began to grasp the profound subtlety of Christ's
teachings against offending our brother; too often our contempt boils down to the fact that we simply disagree with
our brother's position.

Jesus tells us to initiate reconciliation under these circumstances for the same reason he tells us to forgive without
measure: because he knows that much of the time we are too
blind to recognize that we've genuinely hurt someone. The
rationale for seeking forgiveness flows from his great double
commandment: Love God with all your heart and mind and
soul, and your neighbor as yourself.

## PRACTICE

Today, think about the people in your life who might be angry with you for whatever reason. It does not matter if you feel their wrath is undeserved. Choose one of them to approach, pray for wisdom and insight, and then, when you feel ready, call or make your visit in person. You may be utterly amazed at the response.

> Whoever has my commandments and observes them is the one who loves me. (Jn 14:21)

# Day Six: Forgive Someone

*Abba Agathon was asked how sincere love for one's neighbor might be made manifest, and this blessed man, who had attained to the queen of the virtues to a perfect degree, responded: "Love is to find a leper, to take his body, and gladly to give him your own."*[10]

## MEDITATION

Six months before we started building our new house, we had to prepare the site. Though Mike, with the help of his buddies, was determined to do as much of that as he could, we ended up hiring a backhoe operator and a professional tree crew to take down some pines that were just too huge for the buddy crew.

I understood about the pines—the site needed opening up—but I was adamant that we should keep the biggest of them all, a magnificent specimen that matched the one beside my writing studio. They were a pair; they'd been together for who knew how many years; if we took it down, we'd be removing one of the most beautiful trees on the property.

Mike was equally adamant that the pine had to go. First, he tried fear tactics: "It's a hazard," he said. "One good wind, and we'd have a three-hundred-pound branch sticking through our new roof." When that failed to move me, he suggested that the county building department might not give us a permit for the site if they saw how close the big pine stood. Stubbornly, I held out, even when he theorized that the new house would never pass the required fire inspection with that huge mass of flammable timber looming above it.

Though I suspected he was right on all counts, I simply could not bear to see the tree cut down, and eventually Mike dropped the subject. Even though the buzz of the chain saws and the growl of the backhoe went on and on, I assumed my favorite pine would be spared—that he would never give the order to cut it down without my first agreeing to it.

But I was wrong. One morning as I worked in the garden, I happened to glance toward the back of the property just as the first enormous branch came crashing to the ground. A guy hung halfway up the massive trunk in a rope sling, and he was already making serious headway on branch number two. My tree was clearly doomed.

I felt as though I'd been punched in the gut. How could Mike do this to me? I couldn't bear to watch and, shaking with a complicated mixture of sorrow and anger, got in the car and began driving. The longer I drove, the more my conviction grew: I could no longer be married to a man who would cut down a tree I loved this much.

In time, I came to my senses, stopped at church, and knelt in a pew where I tried to pray. Nothing. It was as though my relationship with God had been flash-frozen just like my marriage. And suddenly I became afraid: this powerful anger had cut me out of the herd and was driving me toward the edge of a cliff. While it was in charge of me, I couldn't even cry out for help. Mike was not the problem; anger was.

Jesus was well aware that, when we are this enraged, we are "beside ourselves"—no longer capable of rational thought or loving action. We cannot even pray, and thus we are left wide open to the most hideous suggestions of the Evil One. People in towering rages commit murder. Kneeling in that church, shaking with hurt fury toward my loving, loyal husband, I saw for the first time that anger can literally make us crazy.

But then I saw a life rope dangling before my eyes: Jesus' injunction to forgive, without exception, those who have hurt us. I'd always thought this command a harsh one, impossible to follow. After all, there were moral monsters who did such terrible things that forgiving them felt like condoning evil. And what about justice? How could it be just to forgive those who perpetrated atrocities?

Now, however, I saw what he'd been up to: Jesus knew that, if it were up to us to judge who deserved forgiveness and who did not, few of us would forgive at all. Instead, we'd cherish our self-righteous rage, nurture our towering anger, and soon find ourselves on the road to self-destruction or mayhem. We cannot be trusted to pick and choose whom we will forgive. And so, as followers of Christ, we are enjoined to forgive without measure.

Relieved, I turned my anger over to God and headed home. Every time I looked at the place my tree had stood, I felt weepy. But letting go of the rage allowed me to admit to myself that Mike had been right all along: that magnificent pine had to go. I was not quite ready to say this out loud, of course—in many ways, pride is far more stubborn than fury—but calming down allowed me to face Mike without launching the verbal attack he was no doubt expecting. I could see the relief in his eyes, and I suddenly realized he'd been just as upset about having to thwart my wishes as I was at having them thwarted. He loved me, and he hated having to hurt me. Forgiving allowed me to finally see that.

## PRACTICE

Today, think of someone who has hurt you, betrayed you, or made you angry. You might meditate on an old wound, never healed, or a secret sorrow you've never shared out loud before. Pray about your hurt; ask God to relieve you of the anguish. Then pray for the person who precipitated your pain. If it is still impossible for you to forgive, then pray for the desire to forgive.

Realize that your anger is in some way holding you hostage and that Jesus is offering you liberation if you can only surrender it up to him. Pray to be freed and, in turn, to set free the person you have chained within your unforgiving heart.

> If you forgive others their transgressions, your heavenly Father will forgive you. But if you do not forgive others, neither will your Father forgive your transgressions. (Mt 6:14–15)

# holy week:
## SIMPLIFYING PRAYER

The goal of the desert life was unceasing prayer. The rigorous practices undertaken by the desert dwellers were all in service of developing a single-pointed focus on God.

## Monday: Go to Confession

*Abba Mios was asked by a soldier: "Father, God then accepts the repentance of the sinner?"*

*The Elder, after counseling him with many instructive words, suddenly asked him: "Tell me, my beloved, when you tear your uniform, do you throw it away?"*

*"No," the soldier answered, "I sew it and use it anew again."*

*Then Abba Mios also thoughtfully told him: "If you take pity on your clothing, will not God take pity on His own creation?"*[1]

### MEDITATION

One of the loneliest times in our marriage came hard on the heels of my entry into the Catholic Church. For some years afterward, Mike and I seemed to be standing on opposite sides of an unbridgeable chasm, each bravely trying to shout across the gulf but, most of the time, unable to hear one another. Shortly after the tragic killings at Columbine, however, he announced that he wanted to start coming to Mass with me. As he put it, "There are so many terrible things going on these days—I just want to be with people who are trying their best to be good."

Within a year, he had signed up for RCIA (Rite of Christian Initiation for Adults) and was studying with a group of catechumens seeking to join the Church. Within another year, he was beaming at me from the steps of the altar on the night of Easter Vigil. Before he could officially enter the Church, however, he had to make his first confession.

He chose to do this at a pre-Easter Reconciliation Mass during which ten priests set up temporary confessionals in various parts of the sanctuary. From my spot in line, I could see across the darkened church to where he waited his turn. I knew he was nervous—people who haven't been raised with confession are understandably skittish about articulating their sins to an audience—but I could also tell he was excited.

This was his chance to be released from some painful guilt, to be officially absolved and reconciled with God. I remembered my own first confession ten years before, made to my French Canadian monk friend, Fr. Bernard; it had taken two whole hours of walking down the mountain road and back up again to get only part of it said. I wondered how Mike was going to pull off such a lengthy recitation in such a crowded church. Maybe he was carrying a list?

But when his turn finally came, it seemed as though he'd no sooner sat down before the priest than he was bouncing up and heading back to his place in the pews. I couldn't imagine what had happened, but I knew I couldn't ask: it was his confession after all, not mine. As we got into the car to head home, however, he remarked, "That was great! Not as hard as I thought it would be!"

"Good! Though it seemed kind of . . . short."

"Oh," he said, "well, I figured that, for the first time around, I'd just hit the high points. So I told him that I used to think my dad was God."

I sat back in the seat, amazed. For a first confession, he couldn't have gotten closer to the heart of the matter: I am the Lord your God and you shall have no other gods before me. "Wow," I said finally. "The old idolatry problem. That's a great insight all right."

He nodded, pleased. And I could tell by the look on his face that he'd just been freed from a heavy burden. For, though by now he was long past it, those years of worshipping his father had not only skewed his perception of God but also made it difficult to believe at all. No wonder he hadn't been able to go to church.

The *Catechism of the Catholic Church* explains what happens during confession:

> "The whole power of the sacrament of Penance consists in restoring us to God's grace and joining us with him in an intimate friendship." Reconciliation with God is thus the purpose and effect of this sacrament. For those who receive the sacraments of Penance with contrite heart and religious disposition, reconciliation "is usually followed by peace and serenity of conscience with strong spiritual consolation."[2]

More, the sacrament of Penance restores broken "fraternal communion," or disruption of our relationship with other believers in the Church. And this was, for me, the most profound effect of Mike's first confession: the closing of that great gulf between us and the reestablishment of true intimacy.

For Mike's first confession not only prompted a major insight into his past problematical relationship with God, it gave me a revelation about my own tendency toward idolatry—in this case, a temptation to idolize our marriage. I saw that, if we were going to move closer to God, we had to put our relationship with one another into its rightful place: beneath the sheltering wings of the Holy Spirit.

### PRACTICE

Today, use what you learned through the examen of conscience to prepare yourself for confession. One way to do this is to consider the Ten Commandments, the Commandments of the Church, the Seven Deadly Sins (lust, gluttony, greed, sloth, wrath, envy, and pride), the Duties of One's State of Life (as listed in the Catholic *Catechism*), and the nine ways of participating in the sins of others. These are meant not to discourage you or cause you to despair but instead to give you a standard by which you can judge your behavior.

Then go to a church where the sacrament of Penance is being offered. Prepare yourself through prayer, meet with the priest, and be as honest and open as you possibly can. Follow up by doing the penance you are assigned.

> And so I say to you, you are Peter, and upon this rock I will build my church, and the gates of the netherworld shall not prevail against it. I will give you the keys to the kingdom of heaven. Whatever you bind on earth shall be bound in heaven; and whatever you loose on earth shall be loosed in heaven. (Mt 16:18–19)

## Tuesday: Read a Book or Listen to a Tape about Meditating Today

*One of the elders said: It is not because evil thoughts come to us that we are condemned, but only because we make use of the evil thoughts. It can happen that from these thoughts we suffer shipwreck, but it can also happen that because of them we may be crowned.*[3]

### MEDITATION

The Christian meditation group that meets in our barn each Monday night came into being after I attended a week-end-long silent retreat led by the British Benedictine monk Laurence Freeman. Freeman himself was trained by another Benedictine, John Main. During Main's novice years, he was warned by his superiors not to engage in silent prayer. In the mid-twentieth century, the church had lost touch with its ancient mystical tradition, and the fear was that such practices were more Hindu or Buddhist in nature than they were Christian.

Main reluctantly obeyed the order to cease and desist but continued to read about early monastic practices. Eventually, he discovered a passage written by the fourth-century founder of Western monasticism, John Cassian, that de-scribed to a tee the kind of prayer to which Main was so strongly drawn. In brief, Christian meditation according to Cassian involved sitting still, collecting one's thoughts, focusing on the breath, and silently repeating a single word or phrase. These techniques were not meant to produce some kind of special effect or mystical experience but instead to diminish distractions and help one focus. The goal was greater awareness of God's presence.

The World Community for Christian Meditation grew out of the teachings of Main and his student, Freeman. Active in one hundred sixty countries, it has enabled people in jails and prisons, favelas and slums, and middle-class neighborhoods and wealthy enclaves to learn the basics of contemplative prayer as taught by the Desert Fathers and Mothers. Our Monday night group is one of hundreds scattered throughout the country.

When I first began to meditate years ago at the hermitage, I quickly concluded that I was not cut out for this kind of prayer. For one thing, I was far too physical a person to sit perfectly still for a half hour at a time. And I had so many things on my mind—important things, issues I could not ignore. Sitting quietly for a half hour opened a floodgate of thoughts, and the longer I stuck it out, the more overwhelmed I felt. If this was meant to relax me, then something was clearly wrong.

I struggled along for quite a while before I sought out help. Finally, I got up the nerve to talk with some practiced meditators. I also read several good books on the subject. These taught me that my struggle with distracting thoughts was par for the course and that I was to expect a long siege of distractions—possibly for years—before I finally settled in to the practice. Meanwhile, I could learn to deal with this flood of thoughts by using some of the techniques developed by the desert dwellers.

The fourth-century monk Evagrius Ponticus makes a number of recommendations: First, "stand resolute, fully intent on your prayer. Pay no need to the concerns and thoughts that might arise the while. They do nothing better than disturb and upset you so as to dissolve the fixity of your purpose." Second, "strive to render your mind deaf and dumb at the time of prayer and then you will be able to pray." Third, "if you desire to pray as you ought do not sadden anyone. Otherwise you run in vain." Fourth, if you are in conflict with anyone, then "'leave your gift before the altar and go be reconciled with your brother' . . . and then you shall pray undisturbed. For resentment blinds the reason of the man who prays and casts a cloud over his prayer." And finally, "if you know how to practice patience, you will ever pray with joy."[4]

In other words, in order to meditate, we must become better people. At the same time, meditation itself helps form us into new creatures. In this continuously changing flow between striving and receptivity, we are working out our own salvation—undergoing the transformation of soul that Christ has called us to—"with fear and trembling": fear, in the face of genuine mystery; trembling, as in trembling with joy.

The great secret of Christian meditation is that, for good or for ill, our gluttonous, lustful, avaricious, angry, sad, cynical, vainglorious, and prideful thoughts must finally be dealt with, which means that the root of sin must finally be addressed. Afterward, being human, we may indeed go on sinning but with a difference: no longer do entrenched constellations of self-destructive thought have the power to enslave us.

## PRACTICE

To learn meditation is to begin a slow, lifelong process—fraught with setbacks and disappointments—but also sprinkled with breakthrough moments and real revelation. If you have never tried it before, you might talk with an experienced meditator, visit World Community for Christian Meditation websites, or read some of the many introductory books available. Today, choose one of these, go through it slowly, and pray for the ability to set aside any prejudices that might get in your way. If you have read about it, thought about it, and prayed about it, you will know whether or not you are called to practice this ancient Christian way of prayer.

> How narrow the gate and constricted the road
> that leads to life. And those who find it are few.
> (Mt 7:14)

## Wednesday: Pray for Strangers You See throughout This Day

*One of the elders said: Just as a bee, wherever she goes, makes honey, so a monk, wherever he goes, if he goes to do the will of God, can always produce the spiritual sweetness of good works.*[5]

### MEDITATION

For two years after my solo trip around the world, I struggled with the unexpected aftermath: a reassessment of everything I'd once seen as worthy goals for my life. The time alone in exotic places where nobody knew me, much less knew anything about my "accomplishments," had brought me up short. Was I the person I'd always believed myself to be? Or was I instead an ambition-driven, vainglorious woman, who did what she did solely to garner praise?

I could not stop thinking about my Indian driver's prophetic words: "It's a free life." I longed for that freedom, which I'd never before experienced. But what had he meant? Did I really have to give up all my academic and literary aspirations in order to find the peace that passes understanding?

Meanwhile, I had classes to teach and, since my rooms were scattered all over the hilly campus, lots of walking to do. One morning as I headed down the perimeter road, sunk deep in my own preoccupations—Am I supposed to leave this place?—I passed a girl on her way to the dorms. Something in her face arrested me. She looked . . . despairing. That was the only word for it. Hope had fled. She was terrified. And this early in the morning, she should have been headed downhill like I was, toward the classrooms, rather than back to the dorms. Without even thinking about it, I said a quick prayer for her: Dear Lord, whatever's going on, and I don't have a clue, please strengthen and sustain her to bear her heavy burdens.

A moment later, I passed a young couple deep in conversation. If they had an 8:00 a.m. class, they were going to be late. But whatever they were talking about looked more important. Again, almost without thinking, I prayed for them, two twenty-year-olds in love, still several years from being able to make their own adult decisions but clearly needing good counsel.

Then I passed a handsome boy who looked . . . the only word for it was jaded and possibly depraved. He had a weary but malicious air to him, as though he might do damage to someone simply because he was so bored. I thought of Dostoevsky's famous prophecy—without God, everything is permissible. Mentally, I made the sign of the cross and said another prayer.

It appeared that I'd stumbled upon a new discipline: praying for total strangers as I traversed the hills and valleys of the sprawling campus each day. Eighteen thousand students and ten thousand employees are on campus: twenty-eight thousand people to pray for, most of them (I was guessing) not having heard about God and his providential care. Twenty-eight thousand people in need of prayer gave me plenty to do while I was discerning the next step in my life.

And that's what I did: I prayed for strangers, a few each day. In order to do this, I had to look them in the face—study them in a way that some of them noticed. When they did, I smiled, and usually they smiled back, surprised at the friendly interaction on this huge, impersonal campus. The effect on me of praying for these strangers, however, was no doubt far more powerful than anything that might be happening on their end. For each time I prayed for them, I felt my internal struggle—shall I quit or shall I stay?—begin to lessen.

The great secret of monastic life, which on the surface looks like total withdrawal from human society, is that years of solitude, silence, and prayer, if they are undergone in the right spirit, lead to an expanded heart. Thomas Merton says, "Father, I beg you to keep me in this silence so that I may learn from it the word of your peace and the word of your mercy and the word of your gentleness to the world: and that through me perhaps your word of peace may make itself heard where it has not been possible for anyone to hear it for a long time."[6]

Joan Chittister, a contemporary Benedictine, puts it this way: "To the Benedictine mind, life in all its long nights and weary days is something to be praised, death is the rivet of joy, there is no end to the positive. Even life in hot fields and drab offices and small houses is somehow one long happy thought when God is at its center."[7]

This joy is meant to be shared, whether or not people understand where it is coming from. How do we share it? By looking them in the face as they pass us on the street. By smiling at them. And by praying our silent prayers for their relief from pain, for their protection from evil, and for the opening of their hearts to the God who loves them beyond belief.

## PRACTICE

Today, go out into the world—your school, your place of work, the grocery store, and even the freeway (though it's difficult to see people's faces very well without imperiling your driving)—and spend ten minutes praying for the strangers you pass. The prayers can be simple; you can intuit a lot from body language and facial expressions and can attune your prayers to those clues. A good rule of thumb is that everyone, no matter how cheerful looking, bears some measure of pain. Another is that all of us deal with temptations and fears. You can effectively pray about any of these issues for anyone.

When you are done, take a moment to pray for yourself.
How often do we forget that the pray-er needs prayers as
much as anyone else?

> [I was] a stranger and you welcomed me. (Mt
> 25:35)

## Holy Thursday: Develop a Prayer List Today

*While yet a child, Abba Ephrem had a dream and
then a vision. A branch of vine came out of his tongue,
grew bigger and filled everything under heaven. It
was laden with beautiful fruit. All the birds of heaven
came to eat of the fruit of the vine, and the more they
ate, the more the fruit increased.*[8]

### MEDITATION

I have a friend who owns and runs what I consider to
be the best Christian bookstore in the world. The store
was a years-long dream for him but only came about after
a great tragedy ravaged his life. A devout Orthodox Christian, he has become an icon of Christlike love and wisdom
for many people around the world.

I met him some years ago at a big arts and religion conference in Santa Fe, where I was teaching. He had driven many

hours in order to provide conference attendees with several thousand of the finest Christian titles available. I asked his advice, bought a number of books, and chatted with him a few times during the remainder of the conference. Then the event was over, and I headed home.

A year later, when I arrived in Santa Fe for another stint of teaching, there he was, patiently unloading heavy boxes of books from his old, white van. Not expecting him to know who I was—after all, he serves over three hundred customers at this particular conference, not to mention all the other strangers he meets during the year—I stopped to greet him and reintroduce myself.

Not only did he recognize me, he said, "It's good to see you again, Paula."

"I can't believe you remember me," I said. "I mean, it's been a whole year, and we barely talked—"

"Of course I do," he said with a shy smile, continuing to muscle boxes out of the van. "You're on the list of people I pray for every day. Your name comes right after Deborah's." For a moment, I was struck dumb. Then I saw he was serious. Not only did I, a virtual stranger to him, have a place on his list, I had a particular place, one that he visited in prayer every day. Even more amazing was that, for him, this unusual practice was clearly nothing special. For him, daily prayer for other people was simply one aspect of a serious spiritual life.

Like the Desert Fathers themselves, my friend has deliberately taken on a particular spiritual discipline. Praying for people, no matter how lengthy the list, does not sound particularly radical, however, when compared with some of the other ancient practices, from fasting to keeping vigils to endless recitation of the psalms to repetitive manual labor. These more rigorous disciplines often strike the contemporary person as not merely odd but wrongheaded—perhaps even contrary to the gospels. Not only do they raise the specter of "works," engaged in for the purpose of winning points with God, but they seem difficult, purposeless, and unrewarding. After all, doesn't God love us the way we are? Why deny ourselves the joy of passionate living, particularly when it comes to sexuality? Didn't he create us this way? What possible good can come from suppressing our natural desires and passions?

Our modern concern is understandable but misguided. The goal of ancient Christian asceticism was not a stoical passionlessness but instead freedom from the confusion that results when emotions are running the show, as they so often do these days. The desert dwellers believed that constant emotional turmoil muddies the mind and prevents us from seeing clearly. Their sometimes austere practices were aimed at achieving "purity of heart," or a heart cleansed so completely of egotistical passions and desires that it was able to love as Christ loves. The road to such humility and simplicity of being was long and hard, but when genuine love, purged of all self-centeredness, finally flowered, it brought with it great joy.

The saints of the desert were famous for their accepting and nonjudgmental love for all God's creatures. Such love saw beyond appearances and into the hurting hearts of those who came to them for wisdom and advice. Thus, they were able to do and say what was necessary for the salvation of souls. A thousand years later, Richard of St. Victor summed up their penetrating spiritual vision in this way: "Love is the eye and to love is to see."[9]

My immensely learned but completely humble Orthodox friend, through his patient practice of daily prayer for individual people—some of them virtual strangers and most of them completely unaware of what he does—exemplifies the kind of love made possible by purity of heart. And because his heart is pure, I have no doubt that, when he prays for me, he knows just what to ask for.

### PRACTICE

Think about the people in your life who especially need your prayers. The list may be long, but try to select a handful of people who are in particular need for one reason or another. Take this list to your place of prayer and sit with it for a while with your eyes closed and your mind at peace. Then ask God to teach you how to pray lovingly and effectively for these people. When you feel ready, slowly move down the list until you have held everyone there up to the light of his love. Try, if you can, to continue this practice when Lent is over.

> Love one another as I love you. (Jn 15:12)

# CONCLUSION

The forty days of Lenten "recalibration" end in the great Triduum of the Church: the Mass of the Lord's Supper on the evening of Holy Thursday (usually including a foot washing), the memorial of Christ's passion on the afternoon of Good Friday, and the long wait for the Resurrection during the night of Easter Vigil. At the hermitage, the usual simplicity gives way to Holy Week observances that are as ancient and complex as the Church itself. Even more than during the Divine Office of Ordinary Time, liturgy becomes a magnificent pageant, the acting out of an amazing love story between humanity and the divine. The Easter Triduum highlights the key elements in this story, which also appear as important milestones on our own individual spiritual journeys.

For we, too, must go through a version of Christ's farewell to the world, his death on the cross, and his miraculous resurrection. We do not enter the kingdom on the strength of our professed beliefs alone; we must also undergo preparation, renunciation, and transformation before we are capable of withstanding an intimate encounter with the divine or of responding to God's call to take up his work in the world.

During the Mass of the Lord's Supper, as I watch the
prior kneeling before each of my barefooted brethren with
a basin of water and a towel, I get a taste of Christ's utter
humility—not obsequiousness but rather an immense and
loving strength of purpose. The prior, whom St. Benedict
says is to "play the part of Christ" in the community, reen-
acts on this evening both the pathos of leave-taking—Jesus
is now headed for the cross—and the corresponding joy of
loving servanthood. As he dries their newly washed feet, Jesus explains to his bewildered disciples, "I have given you a
model to follow, so that as I have done for you, you should
also do" (Jn 13:15).

The first lesson I take away from this initial event of the
Easter Triduum is that following Jesus requires that I, too,
must leave the world. By this, I mean that I must be willing
to put God before all other loves, no matter how tender or
urgent. And so, at the beginning of my spiritual life, I must
undergo a wrenching farewell to the way things used to be
and resolutely turn my face toward Golgotha.

The second lesson I absorb is that the path to Christlike holiness is humility. Just as Jesus humbly bore his cross
through the winding streets of Jerusalem, I must be willing
to carry the burden of myself as I am. Instead of fantasizing
about my special gifts or fine character, I must lay aside self-
importance. I must stop catering to my own whims, putting
my own needs before the needs of others, or taking my own

righteousness as a given. I must learn to see myself as I am: neither too high nor too low.

I receive a third lesson during the somber unveiling of the cross on Good Friday afternoon: that renunciation of my former way of life causes suffering, both for me and for those who love me but who are incapable of understanding the journey I am on. No matter how I'd like to avoid that stark reality, what I sign up for when I accept the faith is the quiet bearing of pain. Some of the worst has to do with the total restructuring of the person I've come to identify as myself. Equally hard is to feel old and valued relationships dissolving under the strain of the new.

During Easter Vigil, I learn more difficult lessons yet. As I stand shivering in the foggy darkness outside the hermitage chapel at 3:30 a.m., I have to confront my stubborn individualism—my everlasting temptation to do it "my way." For so many years, this took the form of pitting myself against the church, attempting to be "spiritual" without being "religious." I cherished my aversion to any kind of authority, and I was warily skeptical of the "institutional" nature of Catholicism. At the Easter Vigil, I must confront the fact that genuine transformation requires obedience to a power greater than myself.

I learn another lesson as the monks file out in their white robes and the ancient Vigil bonfire is lit: despite my predilection toward a strictly private relationship with God, I see that we do not and cannot meet him totally on our own. I realize that I am accompanied on this difficult spiritual journey not only by my living brothers and sisters in Christ but also by countless generations of believers who have already made the transition from earthly existence to the "land of likeness"—the heavenly home that Jesus went to prepare for us. No longer merely an individual, I have been engrafted into the Body of Christ.

I get my final lesson as I touch my taper to the fire and take my place in the singing line of oblates, monks, and friends wending their candlelit way into the pitch-dark church. I see that this hard struggle is absolutely necessary. St. Paul puts it this way: "Work out your salvation with fear and trembling. For God is the one who, for his good purpose, works in you both to desire and to work" (Phil 2:12–13). Only when I am willing to renounce my former way of life and my cherished self-identity does the process of transformation begin. And only when I have been changed and made new am I capable of bearing the light of Christ to the world.

The desert dwellers believed the gateway to holiness is prayer without ceasing. God is the source of life, the fountainhead of love, and the fulcrum of power; we stay connected with that source through constant prayer. "Remain in me," Jesus says, "and I will remain in you." But no matter how long and hard we labor, we cannot maintain this connection through our own efforts. According to Jesus, we must instead offer ourselves to God in total humility and openness, like small children, with the diminutive "Abba" on our lips.

In other words, now that we have simplified our space, our marketplace interactions, the care of our bodies, our minds, our schedules, our relationships with other people, and our prayer lives, we must finally ask ourselves about the nature of our relationship with God. Is it as fraught with tension as our reaction to unexpected visitors? Or is it more like an item we no longer use but cannot bring ourselves to discard? Do we see him as a god of x-ray vision, who spends most of his time ferreting out the hidden grime in our lives? Or do we experience him as someone irrationally angry with us for no apparent cause?

The weeks following Easter are a good time to think about our image of God—who we think he is, where we got this notion, and how this or that childish or outmoded view of him might, ironically enough, be getting in the way of our becoming truly trusting and childlike in his presence. When we seriously begin to meditate on our image of God, we are often surprised by how distant, dark, or even frightening it is.

If you find that this is the case for you, the following practices might help. You could choose to try one or more of them during the forty days between Easter and Ascension, or during the fifty days between Easter and Pentecost.

The first, the "practice of the presence of God," was introduced in a brief series of letters by a humble kitchen servant called Brother Lawrence. A lame seventeenth-century monk, he discovered that physical circumstances simply did not matter if he could only remind himself, moment by moment, that he was in the presence of God. You might begin by thinking of God every hour on the hour—or even oftener, as evangelical missionary Frank Laubach, founder of the worldwide organization Laubach Literacy, learned to do despite his exceedingly busy life. In his pamphlet called "The Game with Minutes," he suggested thinking of God for one second out of every sixty as a way to pray without ceasing.

A second practice, meeting God through the beauty of his creation, involves spending time in nature. You might hike or backpack, but there is no need to take such strenuous measures if only you can find a lovely, quiet spot in which to sit and contemplate a tree, a meadow, wildflowers, a stream, or a spectacular display of cumulus clouds. As you look around you, think of the opening passages of Genesis: Let there be light.

If you are a lover of beautiful words, you could try a third practice: reading poetry by artist-believers such as George Herbert, Gerard Manley Hopkins, G. K. Chesterton, Robert Cording, or Mary Oliver, who says very simply, "My work is loving the world."[1] You might write poetry of your own or prayers you have created yourself. You might keep a spiritual journal in which you record special moments of connection with God.

Another practice could be to immerse yourself in images that feed your soul: holy icons, a beautiful exhibit in an art museum, the haunting calligraphy of the St. John's Bible or Barry Moser's woodcuts in the Pennroyal Bible, the color plates in *Image* magazine, or the interiors of cathedrals or modern-day churches such as the ones created by artist William Schickel. You could take an iconography workshop. You might learn to paint with watercolors or oils.

If you are a lover of music, you could make a practice out of listening for the still, small voice of God during the Divine Office at a monastery or on a CD, where the simple beauty of chanting can bring him infinitely closer. You might attend concerts devoted to spiritual works: the cantatas of Bach, Chanticleer's performances of sixteenth-century Mexican liturgical music, Cyprian Consiglio's *Song of Luke*, or the great, old Gospel music artists. Or you could simply sing to God on your own.

Finally, if you are really serious about "simplifying your soul" yet find that a negative image of God is impeding you, you might find a good spiritual director. This search can sometimes be long, but ultimately it will be fruitful if it is conducted primarily through prayer. The desert dwellers believed that those who humbly and sincerely sought guidance would find it but only if they were willing to surrender themselves to the process. A good spiritual director does not have to be a priest or nun but should be prudent, humble, loving, and have the gift of discernment. Sometimes all it takes to finally relinquish a childish and outmoded image of God is the gentle encouragement of a loving guide.

Though the great elders of the desert have long since gone on to meet their beloved Abba, and though living saints are rather hard to come by in our time (though rest assured they most definitely exist), modern technology has given us an unexpected gift: countless translations of ancient contemplative writings that have only become widely available in the past century.

We can, for example, read the *Life of St. Anthony the Great*, one of the first Christian hermits, whose fourth-century biography by St. Athanasius not only helped inspire thousands of would-be hermits and monks to flee the cities and seek solitude in the wilderness but was instrumental in converting the brilliant pagan, St. Augustine of Hippo, to Christianity.

We can study the *Pachomian Koinonia*, which describes the fourth-century establishment of monastic life in the deserts of Upper Egypt. We can delve into the *Institutes and Conferences of St. John Cassian*, whose fifteen-year visit to the great desert elders became the basis for establishing his own monastery in Gaul—and whose work underlies the later Rule of St. Benedict. We can spend time in Evagrius Ponticus's *Praktikos* or study the *Syriac Fathers on Prayer and the Spiritual Life*. In our era, seemingly so disconnected from the great adventure of desert Christianity, we are literally inundated with the literature of holiness. Ironically enough, we now have more access to the wisdom of the desert elders than people have had for seventeen hundred years.

And never have we needed their inspiration more. As Archbishop Anthony of Sourzah puts it,

> We have a great deal to learn from their integrity and their unrelenting courage, from their vision of God—so Holy, so great, possessed of such a love, that nothing less than one's whole being could respond to it. These were men and women who had reached a humility of which we have no idea, because it is not rooted in an hypocritical or contrived depreciation of self, but in the vision of God, and a humbling experience of being so loved.[2]

Of course, our times are not the times of the desert dwellers. The world has changed so dramatically that they would no doubt find it unrecognizable. What has not changed, however, and never will, is human nature. They, and we, were created for the same purpose that Adam was created: to share the divine life with God. For this, we were made in his image and likeness. For this, he sent his son.

Our only way of thanking him is to offer him back what he has so generously given: our consecrated selves. And when we do, we will soon find ourselves carrying out the work for which he fashioned us in our mother's womb. We are made to bring peace to the wartorn, sustenance to the starving, hope to the despairing, love to the despised and the alone, and the good news of salvation to the ignorant and the cynical.

The task sounds daunting but, if not us, who else? We are the workers in the vineyard, the faithful friends that Christ commissioned two millennia ago on his way to the cross. And when we are filled with self-doubt—are we really equipped to do all this?—he reminds us of who he has made us to be:

> You are the light of the world. A city set on a mountain cannot be hidden. Nor do they light a lamp and then put it under a bushel basket; it is set on a lampstand, where it gives light to all in the house. Just so, your light must shine before others, that they may see your good deeds and glorify your heavenly Father. (Mt 5:14–16)

Humility is what allows us to take on this magnificent mission without trembling. And so we go in peace, to love and serve the Lord.

# NOTES

## INTRODUCTION
1. Funk, *Thoughts Matter*, 112.
2. Casey, *Guide to Living*, 28.

## BEGINNINGS: SIMPLIFYING SPACE
1. Merton, *Wisdom of the Desert*, 42.
2. Funk, *Humility Matters*, 22.
3. Chrysostomos, *Flowers from the Desert*, 17.
4. Ibid., 38.
5. Ward, *Sayings of the Desert Fathers*, 73.
6. Quoted in de Waal, *Life-Giving Way*, 124.
7. Merton, *Wisdom of the Desert*, 55.
8. Louf, *Teach Us to Pray*, 10.

## FIRST WEEK OF LENT: SIMPLIFYING THE USE OF MONEY
1. Chrysostomos, *Flowers from the Desert*, 53–54.
2. Caussade, *Self-Abandonment to Divine Providence*, 23.
3. Evagrius Ponticus, *Praktikos*, 31.
4. Ibid., 41.
5. Merton, *Wisdom of the Desert*, 62.
6. Ibid., 60.

7. Quoted in Feiss, *Essential Monastic Wisdom*, 109.

8. Chrysostomos, *Flowers from the Desert*, 37.

9. Quoted in Feiss, *Essential Monastic Wisdom*, 118.

10. Merton, *Wisdom of the Desert*, 33.

11. Belisle, *Privilege of Love*, 27.

12. Ibid., 101.

## SECOND WEEK OF LENT: SIMPLIFYING THE CARE OF THE BODY

1. Ward, *Sayings of the Desert Fathers*, 221.

2. St. Augustine, "The Rule of St. Augustine," Catholicism .org, January 12, 2006, www.catholicism.org/the-rule-of-st -augustine.html.

3. Ward, *Sayings of the Desert Fathers*, 33.

4. Ibid., 209.

5. Casey, *Strangers to the City*, 14.

6. Ward, *Sayings of the Desert Fathers*, 101.

7. Quoted in de Waal, *Life-Giving Way*, 102.

8. Evagrius Ponticus, *Praktikos*, 80.

9. Merton, *Wisdom of the Desert*, 76.

10. Casey, *Strangers to the City*, 89.

11. Evagrius Ponticus, *Praktikos*, 75.

12. Quoted in de Waal, *Life-Giving Way*, 149.

13. Ibid.

## THIRD WEEK OF LENT: SIMPLIFYING THE MIND

1. Chrysostomos, *Flowers from the Desert*, 67.

2. Merton, *Wisdom of the Desert*, 34–35.

3. Evagrius Ponticus, *Praktikos*, 35.

4. Merton, *Wisdom of the Desert*, 30.

5. Quoted in Belisle, *Privilege of Love*, 87.

6. Evagrius Ponticus, *Praktikos*, 36.

7. Fr. Luke Dysinger, O.S.B., "Accepting the Embrace of God: The Ancient Art of *Lectio Divina,*" Saint Andrew's Abbey, Valyermo, last updated December 9, 2005, www.valyermo.com.

8. Chrysostomos, *Flowers from the Desert*, 62.

## FOURTH WEEK OF LENT: SIMPLIFYING THE SCHEDULE

1. Chrysostomos, *Flowers from the Desert*, 76.

2. Kline, *Lovers of the Place*, 96.

3. Merton, *Wisdom of the Desert*, 77.

4. Pieper, *Faith, Hope, Love*, 220.

5. Ward, *Sayings of the Desert Fathers*, 143.

6. Quoted in Belisle, *Privilege of Love*, 87.

7. Russell, *Lives of the Desert Fathers*, 50.

8. Evagrius Ponticus, *Praktikos*, 72.

9. Russell, *Lives of the Desert Fathers*, 77.

10. Quoted in Scott, *Revolution of Love*, 100.

## FIFTH WEEK OF LENT: SIMPLIFYING RELATIONSHIPS

1. Ward, *Sayings of the Desert Fathers*, 133.

2. Cowan, *Desert Father*, 3.

3. Chrysostomos, *Flowers from the Desert*, 33.

4. Kelsey, *Other Side of Silence*, 100.

5. Chrysostomos, *Flowers from the Desert*, 16.

6. Quoted in de Waal, *Life-Giving Way*, 132.

7. Veilleux, *Life of St. Pachomius*, 59–60.

8. Quoted in de Waal, *Life-Giving Way*, 170.

9. Chrysostomos, *Flowers from the Desert*, 89.

10. Ibid., 75.

## HOLY WEEK: SIMPLIFYING PRAYER

1. Chrysostomos, *Flowers from the Desert*, 61.

2. *Catechism*, 1468.

3. Merton, *Wisdom of the Desert*, 45.

4. Evagrius Ponticus, *Praktikos*, 57–58.

5. Merton, *Wisdom of the Desert*, 71.

6. Quoted in Feiss, *Essential Monastic Wisdom*, 131.

7. Ibid., 132.

8. Ward, *Sayings of the Desert Fathers*, 59.

9. Fr. John Zuhisdorg, "2nd Sunday of Lent: Collect (1)," Fr. Z's Blog: What Does the Prayer Really Say? March 12, 2006, http://wdtprs.com/blog/2006/03/2nd -sunday-of-lent-collect-1.

## CONCLUSION

1. Oliver, *Thirst*, 2.

2. Ward, *Sayings of the Desert Fathers*, xv–xvi.

# BIBLIOGRAPHY

Belisle, Peter-Damian, ed. *The Privilege of Love: Camaldolese Benedictine Spirituality*. Collegeville, MN: Liturgical Press, 2002.

Burton-Christie, Douglas. *The Word in the Desert: Scripture and the Quest for Holiness in Early Christian Monasticism*. New York: Oxford University Press, 1993.

Casey, Michael. *A Guide to Living in the Truth: Saint Benedict's Teaching on Humility*. Liguori, MO: Liguori, 1999.

———. *Strangers to the City: Reflections on the Beliefs and Values of the Rule of Saint Benedict*. Brewster, MA: Paraclete Press, 2005.

*Catechism of the Catholic Church*. Liguori, MO: Liguori, 1994.

Caussade, Father J. P. de, S.J., *Self-Abandonment to Divine Providence*. Translated by Algar Thorold. Rockford, IL: Tan Books, 1959.

Chrysostomos, Archbishop of Etna, trans. *Flowers from the Desert: Sayings on Humility, Obedience, Repentance, and Love from the Christian Hermits of Ancient Times*. Etna, CA: Center for Traditionalist Orthodox Studies, 2003.

Cowan, James. *Desert Father: A Journey in the Wilderness with Saint Anthony*. Boston: New Seeds Books, 2006.

de Vogue, Adalbert. *The Rule of Saint Benedict: A Doctrinal and Spiritual Commentary.* Translated by John Baptist Hasbrouck. Kalamazoo, MI: Cistercian Publications, 1983.

de Waal, Esther. *A Life-Giving Way: A Commentary on the Rule of St. Benedict.* Collegeville, MN: Liturgical Press, 1995.

Evagrius Ponticus. *The Praktikos and Chapters on Prayer.* Translated by John Eudes Bamberger, O.C.S.O. Kalamazoo, MI: Cistercian Publications, 1981.

Feiss, Hugh, O.S.B. *Essential Monastic Wisdom: Writings on the Contemplative Life.* San Francisco: HarperOne, 1999.

Funk, Mary Margaret. *Humility Matters for Practicing the Spiritual Life.* New York: Continuum, 2007.

————. *Thoughts Matter: The Practice of the Spiritual Life.* New York: Continuum, 1999.

Hedges, Christopher. *Empire of Illusion: The End of Literacy and the Triumph of Spectacle.* New York: Nation Books, 2009.

Howard, Thomas. *On Being Catholic.* San Francisco: Ignatius Press, 1997.

Kelsey, Morton. *The Other Side of Silence: A Guide to Christian Meditation.* New York: Paulist Press, 1976.

Kline, Francis, O.C.S.O. *Lovers of the Place: Monasticism Loose in the Church.* Collegeville, MN: Liturgical Press, 1997.

Louf, André. *Teach Us to Pray.* Translated by Hubert Hoskins. Cambridge, MA: Cowley Publications, 1992.

Markides, Kyriacos C. *The Mountain of Silence: A Search for Orthodox Spirituality.* New York: Image, 2001.

May, Gerald. *Addiction and Grace: Love and Spirituality in the Healing of Addictions.* San Francisco: HarperOne, 1991.

Merton, Thomas. *Life and Holiness: Merton's Practical Guide to Holiness in the Workaday World.* New York: Image Books, 1964.

———, trans. *The Wisdom of the Desert: Sayings from the Desert Fathers of the Fourth Century.* New York: New Directions, 1960.

Oliver, Mary. *Thirst: Poems.* Boston: Beacon, 2006.

Picard, Max. *The World of Silence.* Wichita, KS: Eighth Day Press, 2002.

Pieper, Josef. *Faith, Hope, Love.* San Francisco: Ignatius Press, 1997.

Postman, Neil. *Amusing Ourselves to Death: Public Discourse in the Age of Show Business.* New York: Penguin, 2005.

Russell, Norman, trans. *The Lives of the Desert Fathers: The Historia Monachorum in Aegypto.* Cistercian Studies 34. Kalamazoo, MI: Cistercian Publications, 1980.

Scott, David. *A Revolution of Love: The Meaning of Mother Teresa.* Chicago: Loyola Press, 2005.

Springsted, Eric. *Simone Weil.* Modern Spiritual Masters. Maryknoll, NY: Orbis, 2002.

Stewart, Columba. *Cassian the Monk.* Oxford Studies in Historical Theology. New York: Oxford University Press, 1998.

Veilleux, Armand, Monk of Mistassini, trans. *The Life of Saint Pachomius and His Disciples.* Vol. 1, *Pachomian Koinonia.* Cistercian Studies 45. Kalamazoo, MI: Cistercian Publications, 1980.

Ward, Benedicta, S.L.G., trans. *The Sayings of the Desert Fathers: The Alphabetical Collection.* Cistercian Studies 59. Kalamazoo, MI: Cistercian Publications, 1975.